BLACK BELT
CROSSWORDS

EDITED BY RICH NORRIS

MARTIAL ARTS CROSSWORDS
SUPER TOUGH

PUZZLE
WRIGHT
PRESS

New York

**PUZZLE
WRIGHT
PRESS**

New York

An Imprint of Sterling Publishing
387 Park Avenue South
New York, NY 10016

PUZZLEWRIGHT PRESS and the distinctive Puzzlewright Press logo are
registered trademarks of Sterling Publishing Co., Inc.

The puzzles in this book were originally published in the Los Angeles Times from 2000 to 2007 and
appeared in the "Los Angeles Times Crosswords" series by Sterling Publishing Co., Inc.

ISBN 978-1-4549-1084-8

Distributed in Canada by Sterling Publishing
c/o Canadian Manda Group, 165 Dufferin Street
Toronto, Ontario, Canada M6K 3H6
Distributed in the United Kingdom by GMC Distribution Services
Castle Place, 166 High Street, Lewes, East Sussex, England BN7 1XU
Distributed in Australia by Capricorn Link (Australia) Pty. Ltd.
P.O. Box 704, Windsor, NSW 2756, Australia

For information about custom editions, special sales, and premium and corporate purchases,
please contact Sterling Special Sales at 800-805-5489 or specialsales@sterlingpublishing.com.

Manufactured in the United States of America

2   4   6   8   10   9   7   5   3   1

www.puzzlewright.com

CONTENTS

INTRODUCTION

Welcome to "Black Belt Crosswords," the fourth in a four-book series designed to increase your crossword skills (or help you brush up on the basics). Either way, you are in for something very special.

The 88 puzzles that follow first appeared on Saturdays in the Los Angeles Times and were edited by crossword sensei Rich Norris. They've been selected for their clever cluing and fresh vocabulary, and every puzzle has been calibrated to provide an extreme mental workout.

One you've earned your black belt in crosswords (by finishing every puzzle in this book), you'll be ready to tackle other Puzzlewright titles like "Tough & Tougher Crosswords" or our "Absolutely Nasty Crosswords" series.

Happy solving!

1

by Harvey Estes

ACROSS
1 Now and then
8 Now and then
15 Unsophisticated
16 Ease
17 Brush component
18 Using few words
19 Cause of Apr. angst
20 Fish in a can
22 Candle count, often
23 Has to spend
25 Wearies
26 Make ___ dash
27 "I'm not ___
   complain ..."
29 Family member
30 Dwelling
31 Sam Snead
   trademark
33 Gets up
34 Appearance
35 Preconception
36 Like many an inn
39 Curfew inspection
43 Taking advantage of
44 Place for a prayer
45 "Love Story" author
46 Gillette razor
47 Old floorboards
   sound
49 Cooked
50 Bro or sis

51 More salty
53 Like Bruckner's
   Symphony No. 7
54 Rearrangement of a
   kind
56 Steers astray
58 Promising
59 Authorize
60 More gracefully
   slender
61 Dump

DOWN
1 White elephants, e.g.
2 Deluge
3 Storm chaser's quarry
4 "___ My Party":
   Lesley Gore hit
5 "Subway Series" team
6 Showy display
7 Union General Philip
8 Joined by treaty
9 Faculty heads
10 Type of squad
11 That, in Toledo
12 Go ape
13 Line with buckets
14 Drops out formally
21 "Doggone!"
24 Endurance
26 Disconcerted
28 Because of, with "to"
30 Aerial defense
   acronym
32 Riled (up)
33 Support

35 Mourned
36 Cosmic rarities
37 "Spartacus" Oscar winner Peter
38 Military operations center
39 "I've ___ had!"
40 Self-centered types
41 Ricotta-stuffed pastry

42 Sneezer's request
44 Simple book
47 Rattletrap
48 Nancy Drew creator
51 Tough kid
52 Speed
55 Hair goo
57 Ballroom bend

2

by Alastair Dusay

ACROSS
1 GYMNAST MILLER
8 Military defense mechanism
15 Sugar, perhaps
16 Diplomatic officer
17 Lobster relative
18 NONSENSE
19 ___ Lingus
20 Detached
22 They may reduce sentences: Abbr.
23 Indication
25 Place in the woods
26 Byzantine emperor known as "the Wise"
29 Ancient gownlike garments
34 James of jazz
37 Wizard revealer of film
39 Attach, as a brooch
40 Cheers from tiers
41 NUN INFLUENCED BY ST. FRANCIS
43 French 101 verb
44 Comprehend
46 Forest denizen
47 Pepsi alternative
48 Bacchic attendants
50 "___ darned!"
52 Tyrrhenian Sea island

54 Cosmonaut's land: Abbr.
57 Masseuse employer
60 Hospital transports
63 "___ Haw"
65 CHAMBERLAIN ROLE
67 School athletic awards
69 Stab
70 Food flatfish
71 Of superior quality
72 Where answers to capitalized clues can be found

DOWN
1 Animal welfare gp.
2 Toasting word
3 Pong maker
4 Naples-to-Cassino dir.
5 Literature Nobelist Gordimer
6 Yemen neighbor
7 Actor Beatty et al.
8 "It Happened One Night" Oscar winner
9 After some delay
10 Fledgling company
11 Spoil
12 Spots in class?
13 Molt
14 Florida ___
21 Emerson, for one
24 Expressionless
27 Non-Rx
28 Electrical unit
30 Reunion attendees

31 Enthusiastic about
32 STOPPER
33 Cut with a knife, old-style
34 Work measures
35 FICTIONAL PLANTATION
36 "How about ___!"
38 City south of Moscow
42 Fish delicacy
45 Introductory, as a sports show
49 Drinking improprieties
51 Hoopla

53 Three-time American League batting champ
55 Biblical queendom
56 Second showing
57 Game with 32 cards
58 Essence
59 Der ___: Adenauer
61 K-12
62 Four seasons
64 Town-line sign abbr.
66 Coming-out party?
68 To the time when, briefly

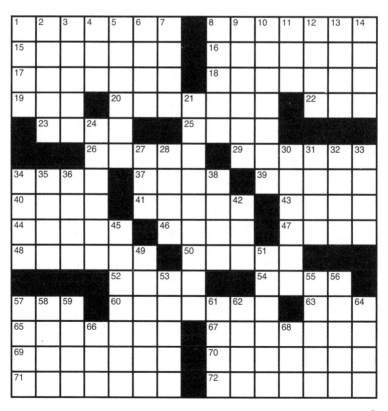

3

by Bob Peoples and Ed Rush

ACROSS
1 Hush-hush terms
10 Shore sound
15 Approximately
16 River through Hypnos's chamber
17 Chat at a reunion, perhaps
18 Aquatic frolicker
19 Din
20 Slough off
22 One way to fly
23 Anderson Cooper channel
24 Optional course
26 Cultivate
27 Narrow escapes
30 Having four sharps
31 Cuts down
32 D.C. wheeler-dealer
33 Amphibian geologic period
35 Stopping, in a way
39 Picnic crasher
40 Bookmaker's bane
41 Steer beef?
42 Wedding music makers
46 Pollster's no.
47 Thumbs-up types?
48 Shout of surprise
49 Small case

50 Space
52 Passport endorsements
54 Gillette razors
56 Rumor conduit
58 Tubular pasta
59 Statement
60 Bean of "To Tell the Truth"
61 Separated

DOWN
1 Snack food staple
2 Like many debates
3 Tyrannize
4 Sister of Ares
5 Fade away
6 Shikoku sash
7 Lew Archer creator MacDonald
8 Royal title
9 Addison's publishing partner
10 Pavement caution
11 Negotiation opener
12 Emperor under Pope Innocent III
13 Help the librarian
14 Role models
21 Loot
25 Some majors
27 Grain-eating bug
28 Jacket material
29 Possess
34 He knocked out Walcott in 1952

35 James's "East of Eden" role
36 Majestic
37 "Impossible"
38 Deteriorate
40 Lake Tahoe and others
42 Bargain-basement

43 One may be designated
44 Road maneuvers
45 Low-heeled shoe
51 Damon or Dillon
52 Aloe ___
53 Novelist Turgenev
55 Washington VIP
57 According to

4

BY HARVEY ESTES

ACROSS
1 Hat attachment
8 Call a spade a heart?
15 Blatant deception
16 Trading places
17 Uses a tickler file, say
18 Newswoman Barbara
19 Ballpark figure
20 Ballpark figure
22 Complexity
23 Former Hart cohost
24 Miles away
27 "We ___ please"
30 Selfish act
33 Security device
38 "Hamlet" Oscar winner
40 "Don't count on it"
41 "Call of the Canyon" author
43 Encroachment
44 Bodybuilder
46 Ages
47 Verbal nudge
50 Camelot, to Arthur
53 Desert danger
56 Compass pt.
59 Winning steadily
60 Endure successfully, as a storm
62 Harrison's "Working Girl" costar
63 More concise
64 Promised
65 World's third-longest river

DOWN
1 Hose shade
2 "Can I get a word in?"
3 Cloverleaf feature
4 Calendar abbr.
5 "Blue Sky" Oscar winner
6 Total
7 Old coin of Cádiz
8 Litter noise
9 "___ the end of my rope!"
10 Cleave
11 "Get somebody else"
12 Geometry calculations
13 Gaiety
14 Slacken
21 Liner, for one
22 Shot from a tee
24 All-inclusive expression
25 "Deck the Halls" segment
26 Similar
28 ___ school
29 Actress Hatcher
31 From dusk to dawn
32 "Pretty Woman" star
34 Seraglio
35 Melville work
36 Bit of shark business
37 Tips
39 "Losing My Religion" band

42 Story
45 In the neighborhood
47 Judging group
48 Trite
49 Valuable violin
51 "Ran" director Kurosawa
52 Escorted, as from
another room

53 Easy win
54 Sculptor Nadelman
55 Transport using runners
56 Low
57 Port on its own gulf
58 To be, in Burgundy
61 Neurologist's order,
briefly

5

BY ELIZABETH C. GORSKI

ACROSS

1 Egyptian talisman
7 Hearts, e.g.
15 Checker of fame
16 Campus figure
17 Element discovered in 1898
18 Despotic
19 MacGraw and others
20 Patron saint of girls
22 When repeated, a Hawaiian food fish
23 Theater area
24 Have a bug
25 John, for one: Abbr.
26 "Serendipities" author
27 White-wine cooking liquids
31 Donations
32 Bit of calligraphy
34 Engelbert Humperdinck hit
36 Yttrium oxide, for one
38 Flower child's accessory
41 Auditions (for)
45 Lyric poems
46 Basic food item
48 Japanese drama
49 DJ's assortment
50 Want-ad abbr.
51 "___ Man": 1965 hit
52 Delivery org.
54 Boy of comics
57 Eastern leader
58 1984 Steve Perry hit
60 Albanian capital
62 Ristorante desserts
63 Money changer?
64 Jam durations?
65 Court break

DOWN

1 Rubs the wrong way, maybe
2 Mass cup
3 Feared fed
4 Sluggers' stats
5 ___ Dhabi
6 One way to deliver
7 First child
8 Peak
9 Emulates L.L. Cool J
10 '50s monogram
11 Wheat ___
12 Genial
13 1996 Summer Olympics star
14 Overshadow
21 Eye angrily
24 Jennifer Saunders's BBC sitcom, briefly
28 "___ hand?"
29 Held firmly
30 Sun. address
31 Tennis legend
33 Makes mad
35 Up ___
37 Legal matter

38 Swarming insects
39 It's useless without its mate
40 Evening service
42 Bring to life
43 Masquerade items
44 Generous types
47 Hang out

53 JFK sights
54 "The Flintstones" pet
55 Get ___ the world: succeed
56 Capone foe
57 Skater Heiden
59 Miss Piggy's query
61 Ox chaser?

6

BY HARVEY ESTES

ACROSS

1 Defeat
5 Oil source
10 Overcharge, in slang
14 Belief
15 Author of didactic stories
16 Vogue rival
17 Flee
18 "Lemon Tree" singer Lopez
19 High-strung
20 Pipe joint
21 Pipe joint?
23 Strident
25 Show of affection
26 Ex-coach Parseghian
27 After a long wait
28 Strangled
30 Makes up for campus partying, maybe
31 Stately dance
32 Thornfield Hall governess
33 Tree trunks
34 Big name in elevators
38 Stinger ingredient
40 "What's your ___?"
41 Morally uncertain subject
44 Capital in Prickly Pear Valley
45 Dusk, to Donne
46 Needing salt, perhaps
47 Fatigue
48 Psychologist's tool
51 Born
52 Skyrocket
53 Doesn't keep from slipping
54 It may be pitched
55 Charter
56 Like "The X-Files"
57 Float component
58 Kazakhstan sea
59 Ships
60 Scottish Reformation leader John

DOWN

1 Musician with a brother named George
2 Blind reverence
3 Kind of phone
4 Krazy of comics
5 Didn't play
6 Tea flavorings
7 Luzon locale
8 Quasimodo portrayer
9 Philosopher who espoused simple pleasure
10 Dates
11 Dated
12 Former White House name
13 Entry device
21 Chuck

22 Nasty sort
24 Acquired
28 Costar with Jane, Laraine, etc.
29 "Lawrence of Arabia" actor
31 Revenue source
33 Supermarket lines?
35 Get loaded
36 Derogatory implication
37 Paycheck reduction for most
39 Bus alternative

40 Chipper
41 Kyoto companion
42 Friend of Monet
43 Capital south of the Black Sea
44 Shows disapproval, in a way
47 Moderate
49 "Seasons in the Sun" songwriter
50 On the fence
54 Condescending cluck

7

by David J. Kahn

ACROSS

1 Do some dueling
12 With regularity
15 Boris Karloff Broadway role
16 City on Guanabara Bay
17 "Sunflowers" setting
18 Campus climber
19 Act dizzily
20 Needle site
21 Saw
23 "Miserere," for one
25 Overfill
27 Contemptible types
29 '50s pol. monogram
31 Part of a routine, maybe
33 Frat letter
36 "Not ___ care"
38 ___-garde
39 She lost her head in 1793
42 Minute
43 Paganini's birthplace
44 One of a lacrosse pair?
45 Kind of reaction
47 Chill
49 Media slant
50 Materialize with effect
52 Brazilian dance
56 "Can ___ witness?"
58 Tailor's concern
60 Swedish chemistry Nobelist Onsager
61 Half a laugh
62 Pony paths
65 Statute
66 Language expert
67 Affirmative
68 Church counter

DOWN

1 Steep slope
2 Pottery and such
3 Cop ___
4 "A Streetcar Named Desire" role
5 Begets
6 Happy Loman's brother
7 Strip of gear, as a ship
8 She lost her head in 1793
9 "___-Tiki"
10 Settle
11 Just made, with "out"
12 Start
13 Automat fare of old
14 Diversion
22 Well partner?
24 1908 Siberia lander
26 Work party
28 Some Art Deco collectibles
30 '50s song syllable
32 Hawaiian verandas
33 Thompson et al.
34 Stringed instrument feature

35 High-intensity lamps
37 Prefix with plasty
40 Goodnight girl of song
41 It's charged
46 Silent steamer
48 Asgard structure
51 Robin's creator
53 Craze

54 French ___
55 Orgs.
57 Cookbook abbr.
59 1998 Australian Open winner Korda
61 Cut grass
63 "___ Believer"
64 Women's follower?

8

BY ALASTAIR DUSAY

ACROSS
1 It's often broken gently
8 "The Screwtape Letters" author
15 Fundamentally
16 Like Simba
17 Seafood delicacy
18 Loser
19 Old TV knob abbr.
20 Wren creation
22 Braggart's suffix
23 Lizzie Borden's sister
25 Long periods
26 "___ Alibi": Selleck film
27 Heads with lists
29 "___ ride?"
32 "Wheel of Fortune" buy
33 Expect
35 Be revolting?
37 Rigging support
40 Fields
41 Troubled state
42 Bar serving
43 Local mail ctr.
44 Veld grazer
46 Boat-lowering device
50 Chucklehead
51 Son of Jacob
53 1964 British Open champ Tony
54 Companion of to
55 Damsels
58 45, for one: Abbr.
59 Vocabulary
61 Discussed
63 Sussex social worker
64 At the movies, maybe
65 Parents
66 Like flowers

DOWN
1 Hit hard
2 Back from shopping, say
3 Jenna Elfman TV role
4 Nancy Drew's beau
5 Headphones, slangily
6 Composed, in a way
7 Hurry
8 Formal provision
9 Advice from a bear
10 Deprivation
11 David Bowie collaborator
12 Asta was one
13 To some degree
14 Guards
21 Work without ___
24 "What's in ___?"
28 Buckle opening?
30 Con
31 Cabbage attacker
34 City SE of Turin
36 Kind of artery
37 Contest using a rope
38 Released conditionally
39 Hypothetical, as financial statements
40 Pot spot

42 Flew
45 Electrician's tool
47 Springlike
48 Ascribe
49 Patted down
52 Fatuous
55 Thick hair
56 Golden ___
57 Game with no card lower than seven
60 "Golden," in a Rimsky-Korsakov title
62 Author LeShan

9

by Raymond Hamel

ACROSS

1 It's broken when it's used
4 Bladder
7 Hot stuff
12 Champagne bucket, e.g.
13 1982 Disney film
15 Elite group
16 Manny of baseball
17 A, in communications
18 Open plain
19 Film ending on the Statue of Liberty
22 Erect
23 Violinist Mischa
24 Faithful follower
27 Lay one's hands on
31 Flightless bird
33 Pro ___
35 Cuba ___
36 Maker of a popular catalog
39 Remaining
40 Saperstein and Vigoda
41 Nuts or bananas
42 Battling
44 City south of Clearwater
46 View from the Left Bank
48 It's commonly twisted
52 1976 U.S. Medal of Freedom recipient
57 Measure
58 Solitary
59 "Dies Irae," e.g.
60 Put in prison
61 Mother ___
62 Eye piece
63 Shadowboxes
64 English dramatist Thomas
65 NFL stats

DOWN

1 Paris's ___ des Beaux-Arts
2 Imply
3 It's served in a bowl
4 Hits or runs
5 Woody's boy
6 It's often oversized and illustrated
7 Easy to peddle
8 Harper's Magazine rival, with The
9 Sudden transition
10 Normal
11 Old Testament prophet
12 Mischief-makers
14 Part of NASDAQ: Abbr.
20 Prefix with cardial
21 Med. plan choice
25 Lapse
26 Greek goddess of the earth
28 Julie's "East of Eden" role

29 Peeved
30 Catch, in a way
31 Kitchen protection
32 Siete follower
34 Sailing
36 Intl. broadcaster
37 Diners, at times
38 Ukr., once
43 Recruit's sentence ender

45 Hot air
47 Lacking value
49 Entered
50 Describes
51 River to the Danube
52 A long time
53 Stadium entrance
54 Sousaphone cousin
55 May race, familiarly
56 Sine qua non

10

BY MARTIN
ASHWOOD-SMITH

ACROSS

1 Embargos, blockades, etc.
16 Squash variety
17 Really limber
18 Pro with a pad
19 Its force is measured in megatons
20 Not obvious
21 ___-mo replay
23 Remnant
24 Liq. measures
27 Type widths
29 Assn.
30 Cotswold cry
33 Ishmael's overseer
35 Gray matter site
38 Office installation
40 Better
41 Entr'___
42 "Losing My Religion" band
43 Old TV part
44 Globe
46 Brooding type?
47 ___ kwon do
48 Down
50 Hot glower
53 Light lead-in
56 Indian term of respect
60 Sell well
63 Leave the pen, say
64 Friendly pact

DOWN

1 Bartok and Braun
2 "___ Si Bon": 1950 song
3 Rude look
4 Dodge models
5 "Becket" actor
6 ___ in Mike
7 Doubter's words
8 Kin group
9 Set point?
10 G.P.'s gp.
11 With anger
12 Fern leaf
13 The King's middle name
14 Went higher
15 Washstand accessory
22 Like some breezes
23 They're opposite points
24 Persian Gulf nation
25 Melodic subject
26 "The Crucible" setting
28 Athletics
29 "You're ___ talk!"
30 Fluff
31 Rocky ridge
32 Clio winners
34 Sound unit
36 Jam or pickle preceder
37 Lee side?: Abbr.
39 Vagabond
45 Sewn, in a way

47 Lead-and-tin alloy
49 "___ suggest ..."
50 Outer limit
51 Pained cry
52 Lure
53 Balsa, e.g.
54 Ill. neighbor

55 Skinny, so to speak
57 "If I ___ Hammer"
58 Hot star
59 "Let it ___": Everly Brothers hit
61 Small crawler
62 Boxer's warning

11

BY HARVEY ESTES

ACROSS

1 In formation
8 Information
15 Flowerlike marine creature
16 Driver's option
17 Noted gateman
18 Valkyries, e.g.
19 Big name in catalogs
20 Unwilling words
22 Slope slider
23 European hub
24 ___Kosh B'Gosh
25 Stand for a sitting
27 Poet's palindrome
28 Can't stand
31 Tramp lover
32 Amount to take
34 Flower feature
36 Flight that always arrives early?
40 Crack
41 Ballpark figure
43 Stage accessory
46 Honorees' spots
48 One of a pack, perhaps
49 Car starter?
51 "AC360" channel
52 Speech hurdle
53 Entrance requirements for some

54 Plumed military hat
57 Cellist Casals
58 Itinerant
60 Place for free spirits?
62 Accept blame quietly
63 Kind of store
64 Rely on implicitly
65 Realms

DOWN

1 Roped
2 Petrified
3 Sherpas, e.g.
4 Board abrasive
5 Die markers
6 One in France
7 "... shall not ___ from the earth": Lincoln
8 Mahayana master
9 Arabian sultanate
10 Decide to forget, with "off"
11 Pop
12 "Battleship Potemkin" setting
13 Flirted subtly
14 With meddlesome intent
21 You can't eat with just one
24 Observed
26 Exhausted
28 Scotch bottle word
29 DDE's party
30 Producer Bochco
33 Get to work, in a way

35 Tops of suits
37 Water-testing org.
38 Makeup artist?
39 Frequent rescuee of fiction
42 Committee output
43 Feline flocks
44 Change, as boundaries
45 Like some training

47 Stuck-up types
50 Moving
52 Knight stick
55 Rosemary, for one
56 Pseudocultural
57 Phnom ___
59 Govt. consumerism group
61 Oomph

12

BY HARVEY ESTES

ACROSS

1 Troublemakers
5 Eateries serving everyone the same fare
15 Brindisi bucks of old
16 Liberty
17 Way out
18 Way out
19 Silver State residents
21 Sell very high, perhaps
22 Sign of a slip
23 Overcharging concern?
25 Small containers
26 Croat, for one
30 Kid stuff
32 Dr. Seuss title character
33 Pink-slip
34 Relative record
35 Like some furniture
36 Kind of film
37 Stadium shout
38 Bored type, maybe
39 Ways
40 Mourned in verse
42 Double agent
43 Didn't just pass
44 Warren's predecessor
47 Ready
50 Holy ___
51 Beginners' book phrase
54 Hubble Telescope builder
55 Ideals
56 Got off
57 Revealing words
58 Nuisance

DOWN

1 "Mr. Belvedere" actress Graff
2 Social
3 Spade, e.g.
4 Reserve
5 Box office boosters, often
6 Arles's river
7 Guitarist Watson and a dwarf
8 Bug
9 Teachers' org.
10 Place for contributions
11 Isn't passive
12 "___ Rock"
13 Superhero's adversary
14 Barely penetrate
20 Shore thing
23 "Four Apostles" painter
24 Richard of "Love Me Tender"
26 Coupled
27 Broward County's ___ Lakes
28 Drive train component
29 Cat scanners?
30 Eye sore
31 River through Orsk

32 Lallygagged
35 Slow flow
36 Hard time to warm up
38 Orders
39 Eighth-century invader
41 Genesis plot
42 Dessert order
44 Engulf
45 Spring site

46 Three-time Emmy winner Jane
47 Shaggy do
48 Inner circle, with "the"
49 Mystery name
50 "___ yellow ribbon ..."
52 "The Simpsons" bartender
53 OR figures

13

BY BOB PEOPLES

ACROSS

1 Kind of cocktail
8 Stockpiles
15 Hot
16 Unruffled
17 Is casually involved
18 Equitably determined
19 Pres. monogram
20 Revealed inadvertently
22 Lamb serving
23 "I forgot the words" syllables
25 Retro photo
26 It's good to go out with one
27 Build
29 First of December?
30 Beatrice's lover
31 It usually requires a signature
34 Nimbus output
35 Pouting, say
41 "___ my case"
42 Some MIT grads
43 Old-time actress June
44 Puts on
45 Nairn knolls
47 Apollo's creator
48 USNA grad
49 Deadline
51 Part of EST: Abbr.
52 Angels, perhaps
54 Herpetologist's subject
56 Con
57 Butcher's tool
58 Lunches and brunches
59 Political aides

DOWN

1 Oft-referenced note
2 How many stunts are undertaken
3 Mailroom machine
4 Sphere
5 Exaggerated
6 Curved moldings
7 Pension plan features
8 Commercial testing, e.g.
9 "West Side Story" song
10 At the summit of
11 Round Table address
12 Deck preserver
13 Diplomatic goal
14 Shock
21 Absorb quickly, in a way
24 Field or Stone
26 Cricket figure
28 Four-time 20-game winner Luis
30 Profundity
32 Spell
33 Mauna ___
35 Feature story supplement
36 Period of metalwork advances
37 Camera accessory
38 Slippery

39 Bird, at times
40 Dealers
45 Sudden outbreak
46 Memorial marker
49 Remote sites?

50 Sport played to three points
53 Korean auto
55 "She's So High" singer Bachman

14

BY DAVID J. KAHN

ACROSS

1 Optimistic conditional
7 Whistle blower
10 Dorm resident, maybe
14 More than words
15 Porter, e.g.
16 Zeno's home
17 Meet again
19 British blackbird
20 Actress Skye
21 Saperstein of Harlem Globetrotters fame
22 Botch
23 Man-mouse link
24 "Sophie's Choice" narrator
26 It may result in overtime
27 Jamaican style
30 Poet Noyes
32 1965 hit by 37-Across
36 Coastal threat
37 See 32-Across
42 Attack
43 Get support from
44 His won-lost record was 56–5
45 Discovers
49 Go after, in a way
50 "Quo Vadis" director
52 Treeless area
53 Crumb
54 Put in a magazine, say
55 It rises in the Valdai Hills
58 Suggestion starter
59 "Got it!"
60 Land development?
61 Game ending
62 Strain
63 Craving

DOWN

1 Conceived beforehand
2 Something to prove
3 "Dead Again" star
4 Facility
5 '60s demonstration target: Abbr.
6 Grass-roots support?
7 Temple prayer
8 Sitcom first called "These Friends of Mine"
9 Charge
10 Rig
11 Dietary fat subsitute
12 Like some allowances
13 Light-headed?
18 Exercise aid
22 "Tartuffe" playwright
24 Like a bread knife
25 Instep coverings
28 Art class
29 Fish out of water
31 Business concerns
33 Urge
34 Anatomical duct
35 Relative of -like

37 Sink the putt
38 Dubai or Ajman
39 "We're through"
40 They give a lot of tips
41 Mock
42 Coloratura legend
46 ___ Bowl

47 Kick back
48 Pester
51 It may come from the fridge
53 "La Bohème" heroine
55 Tub
56 Statute
57 Bowl call

1	2	3	4	5	6		7	8	9		10	11	12	13
14							15				16			
17					18						19			
20					21				22					
23				24			25			26				
27		28	29					30	31					
32				33	34	35								
		36												
37	38								39	40	41			
42						43								
44		45		46	47	48			49					
50		51		52				53						
54			55			56	57							
58			59			60								
61			62			63								

15

BY JAMES E. BUELL

ACROSS

1 Astral
11 Real est. offerings
15 "Così fan tutte," for one
16 Tie
17 It's difficult to be in one
18 Bit of funny business
19 Concern for one who's laid up
20 Vamp victim
22 Insurance subject
24 Most plain
25 Expansion
29 Wasn't serious about
31 One who tears up easily
32 Guinness and others
33 Mex. neighbor
34 Recordholder with 4,256 hits
35 Xylophone sound
36 City near Moscow
37 "Who ___ to argue?"
38 Make
39 Time away from work
40 Ink spot
42 Support beams
43 Memory trace
44 Pond floater
46 Cutting
48 Dwelling support used by primitive whale hunters

53 Comics canine
54 Mudslinging sort
56 Some agents
57 Dextrose
58 Sweat it
59 Pitfalls for those over 65?

DOWN

1 Union opponent
2 Board at the track
3 Surrounded by
4 They're in for the long haul
5 Savant
6 Muscle car
7 Basilica sections
8 Vim
9 Piccadilly Circus statue
10 Be historically traced (to)
11 Request in earnest
12 Courses of action
13 Comes to the table, say
14 Soft-soaps
21 Era
23 Cast relatives
25 Removes with effort, as paint
26 Square dancer, at times
27 Intensifying sentiment
28 Width measure
30 Advance
32 British dramatist Ayckbourn

35 First coats
36 "... ___ quit!"
38 Tusked beast
39 Pretentious speech
41 High ___
42 Pie-eyed
45 Crinkled fabric

47 Cavil
49 Obscure
50 First name in '70s
   Olympics
51 Minimal tide
52 Goes wrong
55 Fannie ___

16

BY DAVID J. KAHN

ACROSS

1 Important area at home
11 Muhammad and others
15 Statute affecting a small group
16 All there
17 Totally outclassed
18 Start of North Carolina's motto
19 Performance
20 Appetizing spreads
22 Maritime dangers
25 Gypsum painting surface
26 Autobiographer Turner
27 Aleppo resident
29 Capital at 12,000 feet
31 Trunk terminus
36 Love, to Luis
37 Super Bowl XXXV champs
41 Peter Fonda title role
42 Romantic gift
43 Digger
45 Some wallpapers
49 Fled
50 16th-century painter Veronese
55 Take ___
56 It involves putting a line through a hole

59 Big ___
60 Prank
61 "Mark Twain and Me" actress
64 Slaughter of baseball
65 Tangy refreshers
66 Family business word
67 Layoff causes

DOWN

1 Stabs
2 Emmy-winner Ullman
3 "Roll, Wagons, Roll" star
4 "___ Gotta Be Me"
5 Great Plains st.
6 List ender
7 Woody Allen title role
8 Oil source
9 Narthex-to-chancel areas
10 Still-life subjects
11 On a galleon, say
12 Application entry
13 Suitable for eating
14 React to a shot
21 D.C. figure
23 Like some sheets
24 It's a wrap
28 Winsor McKay's "little" comics character
30 Shelters
32 Long time
33 Roman crowd?
34 Poet's preposition
35 Can. part

37 Tourist activities
38 "Dick Tracy" actor
39 Pressured
40 ___ Minor
44 Center opening?
46 Reaffirming answer
47 Karan contemporary
48 Management subject?

51 Early fur trader
52 Busy landing place
53 Purplish hue
54 Cat-___-tails
57 Conductor Lukas
58 Sitcom staples
62 Parisian pronoun
63 "Bali ___"

17

BY BOB PEOPLES

ACROSS

1 Filled food
5 Open audition, in slang
15 Harald V's father
16 Hardly a VIP
17 Infrequent
18 Two-hulled vessels
19 Part of AAA: Abbr.
20 Enzyme suffix
21 Resign
22 Nightclub
24 Errant shot
26 Shower time: Abbr.
27 Heat, to a hood
28 Some racing cars
31 Quickly and eagerly
37 1979 V.S. Naipaul novel
38 Scuttlebutt
39 Fizzling sound
40 Accelerator
41 IRS Form 1040 datum
42 Sob
44 Spring break mecca ___ Beach
48 Earns
51 Carrier with its H.Q. in Tokyo
52 The poky
53 Individually
56 Nervous spasms
57 Be awed by
58 Second

59 You don't have to study for it
60 Rounded hammer part

DOWN

1 Ark contents
2 Texan independence landmark
3 They may handle estates
4 Pass the budget
5 Chocolate bean
6 Command to a sailor
7 25-Down source
8 Singing syllable
9 Flight
10 "Holy moly!"
11 Largest known asteroid
12 In ___
13 Actress Anderson
14 For fear that
23 Where many El Grecos hang
24 Dayan of Israel
25 Nice thoughts
27 Babe and others
28 Decide to leave, formally
29 Ring site
30 Spanish painter José María ___
31 Statutes
32 Native Nigerians
33 Depend
34 Draft words
35 Pretentious
36 Baby's milestone

42 Bob's partner?
43 Rob of "Melrose Place"
44 British nobles
45 On guard
46 Special place
47 Torch job
48 Some den leaders

49 Sci. course
50 "From Here to Eternity" actress
51 Kid
54 Leiter and Dark of baseball
55 Add (up)

18

BY HARVEY ESTES

ACROSS
1 Lets go
11 "Let's go!"
15 "A Man and a Woman" actress
16 Perfect
17 Moniker mishap
18 Broadcast
19 Battery abbr.
20 Doesn't work
21 Ho's "hi"
22 Strong dislike
24 Put in a log
26 Dealer's request
29 List of what was missed
30 Course expectations
32 Messing of "Will and Grace"
34 Golf broadcaster Baker-Finch
35 Escape
36 Broadcast
37 Fraternal group
38 Mauna ___
39 Up to
40 Freelancer's encl.
41 Pigment-deficient plant
43 "Pearl Pearl Pearl" guitarist Lester
45 Marathoner's need
47 Came together
51 Knocks down

52 "A Star Is Born" actor
55 Mideast gp. since 1964
56 Tony's cousin
57 Event at which Romeo and Juliet fell in love
59 Caramel-topped dessert
60 Bug fighter
61 Ward (off)
62 Kind of attitude

DOWN
1 Busch Gardens locale
2 It's divided into chapters
3 "Lou Grant" reporter
4 Enthusiast
5 Courses at Vail
6 Current info
7 Works at the Louvre
8 Skip
9 Just know
10 Neurologist's order, briefly
11 Bad temper
12 Features of Disneyland and Seattle
13 Bribable
14 Sparks denizens
21 Razor handle?
23 Emporium
25 Dweeb
27 Revision
28 Letter enhancement
30 Furniture with cushions
31 Willie Mays, for one
33 Ringer in a ring
35 One follower?

36 Presently
37 Grub
39 Les États-___
40 Stunt double, e.g.
42 Loom
44 It multiplies by dividing
46 Range maker

48 Fights
49 "Dallas" matriarch
50 Sweetly, to Solti
53 City SE of Turin
54 Sketch
57 Paw's partner?
58 Spa specimen

1	2	3	4	5	6	7	8	9	10		11	12	13	14
15											16			
17											18			
19			20						21					
22			23				24	25						
			26		27	28		29						
	30	31			32		33				34			
35				36						37				
38			39					40						
41		42			43		44							
45					46			47			48	49	50	
51					52	53	54				55			
56			57						58					
59			60											
61			62											

19

by Bob Peoples

ACROSS

1 Atlas abbr.
4 Champs Élysées feature
8 Lop
14 Greek personification of death
16 Spring bloomer
17 Brass
18 Bit of wisdom
19 Remote arena perspective, facetiously
21 Verbose
22 Even (with)
23 Took in
24 One seeing a lot of red?
25 Evian, e.g.
28 Big Ten footballer
31 Reduces to a pulp
35 Tolerated
36 Some openers
37 Noted advisor
38 "A Perfect Spy" author
39 Antiquity, once
40 Curriculum component
42 Univ. employees
43 Rodeo need
46 Edna O'Brien's "The Country ___"
48 Walk
52 Proof of a kind
53 Vaughan Williams's "___ Antarctica"
55 Precisely
56 Photo lab purchase
57 Obliterates
58 Seaweed derivative
59 Ballpark fig.

DOWN

1 Committee sess.
2 Bernard Malamud novel
3 Instant
4 "Hero" singer, 1993
5 Run ___
6 Conformed
7 Ancient Palestinian
8 Wall St. "500"
9 College town NE of Los Angeles
10 Risk
11 One of Chekhov's "Three Sisters"
12 They're found in yards
13 Dieter's count
15 Capone harasser
20 More than loud
21 Blather
24 Open hearing, in law
25 Like some plans
26 Rah-rah meetings
27 Weigh
29 Floored
30 Squeeze (out)
32 Big name in champagne
33 Bars in markets?: Abbr.
34 RR stop

41 Disgust

43 Future litigators' exams: Abbr.

44 "___ Grows in Brooklyn"

45 Needles

46 Succeed

47 "___ out?": dealer's query

48 Name

49 Carbon dioxide's lack

50 ESPN subject

51 On Ventura Blvd., say

54 Trickery

20

BY BOB PEOPLES

ACROSS

1 IHOP order
8 Trips
15 Not too many
16 Settle
17 Cliché
18 Figures to analyze
19 CD follower
20 Bit of a draft?
21 Some sports cars
22 Thrice, in prescriptions
23 "___ Baby": song from "Hair"
25 Like "The X-Files"
27 N.Y.C. commuter line
28 Far East weights
30 Cartoon chihuahua
31 Baron Munchhausen's chronicler
32 Additional conditions
35 "The ___ File": Deighton spy novel
36 They may follow book reviews
44 Starting gaits
45 Where It.'s at
46 Piece of music
47 Instrument with 10 keys
48 Retro photo
50 CBer's word
51 Seeing red
52 Quarter-mile, maybe
53 Extra effort of a kind
55 "___ Carousel": Hollies hit
56 Struggling
58 First coed college in the United States
60 Orange liqueur cocktail
61 Had vivid memories of
62 Some ads
63 Puppies, often

DOWN

1 Much-studied critters
2 Swinger?
3 More spacious
4 Bubble source
5 Certain Prot.
6 Doo-wop favorite, e.g.
7 Louis Armstrong classic
8 Area of untapped resources
9 Declaim
10 Cries of pain
11 "Your point being ...?"
12 Lecherous
13 Music Muse
14 Had the biggest part
24 Certain Ivy Leaguer
26 Erupts, as in anger
27 Resinous stuff
29 Tizzies
31 Scraping tools
33 Local mail ctr.
34 "Murder in the Cathedral" monogram

36 Democritus, philosophically
37 Pope of 1261-1264
38 Thingies
39 Social finale?
40 "Now I get it!"
41 Turn
42 Harder to see

43 Seashores
48 Set of Muslim prayers
49 "Three Tall Women" playwright
52 Crazy
54 Part of a block?
57 Cool
59 Assail, with "into"

21

BY BRENDAN EMMETT QUIGLEY

ACROSS

1 Group with the album "Significant Other"
11 Work
15 Lack of polish
16 In a class with
17 Ruts
18 Holly genus
19 Artist Warhol
20 Shackle
22 Type of whisper
25 In the thick of
28 Madrid's Puerta del ___
31 Ben follower?
32 Suburb of Cleveland
33 Mariner's dir.
34 "___ Tu": 1974 hit
36 Wide of the mark
37 Zoological openings
38 "Leading With My Chin" author
40 Tramp, briefly
41 Spoke, e.g.
43 Load
44 When the French fry?
45 Edit
46 Athlete's intro?
47 Light color
48 Axle bars that prevent rolling
50 Hope
52 "Popeye" tyke
54 Triumphant exclamations
58 "Off the Court" autobiographer
60 Casual
63 River from Pittsburgh
64 John Hancock site?
65 Head of Germany
66 One who ignores limits

DOWN

1 Type of bean
2 A party to
3 Recover, as from injury
4 Tactics
5 Wager
6 "Can ___ now?"
7 "The Spirit of the Border" author
8 Dog, in some store names
9 Guarantees, in slang
10 Induction motor inventor
11 "Brideshead Revisited" Emmy winner
12 Construction machine
13 Luau instrument
14 ___ object
21 Food of the gods
23 1949 courtroom film
24 Vague emanations
26 Boxer's group
27 Labeled
28 Z's, perhaps

29 Connecting road
30 Head honchos
35 Driver's caution
36 Accustom
39 Dramatic interlude
42 Stunned by
49 E-mails
50 Al ___
51 "My Dinner With Andre" director
53 Lowdown

55 "The Lost Boys" actor Corey
56 Year in old Rome
57 British machine gun
58 Hunky-dory
59 HBO competitor
61 "___ Never Seen Julie Cry": Jo Dee Messina song
62 Put in

22

BY JAMES E. BUELL

ACROSS

1 Ancestor
11 It may be a sore spot
15 Hotel convenience
16 Not
17 Some flights
18 Movie dog
19 Small pies
20 Contribute
22 Mountain road feature
23 Prove competent
24 Spreads out
28 Gas, e.g.
29 Goal
30 Animated character
31 Ornamental case
33 It may be seen around the house
35 Often
36 Shakespeare's Katharina, notably
38 One side of the Urals
39 Spoken for
41 ___-Rooter
42 Musician Lennon
43 Baseball stat
44 Baltic feeder
46 The Windsors, in the news
48 First clothing source?
50 For each
51 Not working, perhaps
52 Decide not to intervene
57 Firenze farewell
58 Toy you blow into
60 Put through the paces
61 Striking
62 Fast fleet
63 Resolute

DOWN

1 Hand ball?
2 Numerical prefix
3 Bring up
4 Issue
5 Granger of "Strangers on a Train"
6 Security concerns
7 "___ the ticket!"
8 Boo relative
9 Ethyl ending
10 Heroic act
11 Spiral-shelled mollusk
12 World's largest inland lake
13 Mock
14 At all
21 Fair share, often
23 Pacify
24 Tell it like it is
25 Opposite conditions
26 Act horrified
27 Upfront payment
28 Uproar
32 Number of Punic Wars
34 Elementary
37 Became harder to tolerate

40 Standard
45 Intensify
47 Actor Bean and novelist Scott Card
49 Cutie pie
50 Linguine topper

52 Sprawled
53 Box
54 "Put ___ my tab"
55 Latin deity
56 Harper's Bazaar illustrator
59 Tokyo, formerly

23

BY BOB PEOPLES

ACROSS

1 Defense attorney's challenge
16 Big name in porcelain
17 College disappointment?
18 Job safety org.
19 See 11-Down
20 Sushi fish
21 IV sites
23 Cal. pages
25 32-qt. dry measure
28 Append
32 An ex of Frank
35 Sound of a slip?
37 "I Have a Rendezvous With Death" poet
39 Is less vigilant
41 Lock trouble?
42 Badger
43 Stallone sobriquet
44 Man on the street
46 "Delta of Venus" author
47 ___ Clemente
48 Abu Dhabi's fed.
50 Obi-Wan's portrayer
53 Subj. usually studied at night
56 Deep cut
59 Attack force at sea
64 1996 bestseller about social policies
65 Oft-unexplored areas

DOWN

1 Get a lode of this
2 Game played on a 300-yard-long field
3 Seers?
4 Cheese holder
5 Hitching posts?
6 M.Sgt., for one
7 19th-century French book illustrator
8 Go over
9 Decided, as a jury
10 German conjunction
11 With 19-Across, famous last words?
12 Sidewalk eateries
13 "Permit Me Voyage" poet James
14 Close up
15 Tolkien creations
22 Act of convincing
23 Love letter phrase
24 Ten C-notes
25 Fall plantings
26 Bar in the water
27 Informal greeting
29 Actor Eric of the 1937 film "Shall We Dance?"
30 Cutty Sark alternative
31 NBA '92-'93 Rookie of the Year
32 "Not ___!"
33 "Rigoletto" composer
34 Warwickshire forest
36 Part of a Homer Simpson snicker

38 Lux. locale
40 Important Indian
45 Shake while in motion
47 Fight
49 Warren and Weaver
50 Kind of rain
51 Held up, maybe
52 Art Deco designer
53 Formerly, formerly

54 Moselle tributary
55 Exist
57 In order (to)
58 Monster, so to speak
60 '50s nickname
61 Some M.I.T. grads
62 Guitarist Ocasek of The Cars
63 Foot, in zoology

24

BY ARLAN AND LINDA
BUSHMAN

ACROSS

1 Diamond figure
8 Decorate
15 Olympics figure
16 South Pacific islands,
collectively
17 Superficial
18 Worship sites
19 Occasionally
21 Echidna morsel
22 Corrida cry
23 Beginning to do
well
27 Winter storm
consequence
30 Movie extra?
33 Carry out
37 Idioms
38 Gay
39 Buying and selling
41 They may be single
42 Beauty pageant elite
44 Explode
47 RMN was his
running mate
50 Plastic ___ Band
51 Dollar figure?
55 Strove for
59 Some paints
60 Spine
61 Orbit

62 Massage target
63 Flinched

DOWN

1 Opera villain, often
2 Dramatist Fugard
3 Disgrace
4 Model Macpherson
5 Disappear, with "away"
6 Yours, in Avignon
7 Freshly cut
8 Became irritated
9 Incomparable service
10 Sleep acronym
11 Forty winks
12 Holiday visitor
13 Tuscany city
14 Rash
20 Close
24 Japanese mercenaries
25 Elbow grease
26 Ranges
27 Pooh-poohs, with "at"
28 Unqualified
29 "Twelfth Night" duke
30 Exactly
31 NHL legend
32 36-Down's org.
34 Start of a dog's name
35 Persian, e.g.
36 Two-time U.S. Open
champ
40 Tape deck component
41 Lobster feature
43 Merino's hangout
44 Talk big

45 Link
46 Common type style
47 "She ___ among the untrodden ways ...": Wordsworth
48 Investigate
49 Moderated

52 Work without ___
53 Island on the Bali Strait
54 Cupid
56 Printing widths
57 Early sixth-century date
58 "Wheel of Fortune" buy

25

BY MANNY NOSOWSKY

ACROSS

1 Carol sequence
7 Added oomph to
15 Arthurian isle
16 Slightly bitter, maybe
17 Past
18 Discuss
19 Muscateer?
20 Reason for bursting?
21 Turkish mount
22 Be unresolved
23 Allowed number
24 Safari sights
25 "Maid of Athens, ___ we part ...": Byron
26 Some are blue
27 Party paper
28 It may be preceded by an aura
30 Dam, e.g.
31 With enthusiasm
32 Tourist attraction in southern Florida
36 Bumped into
37 At top speed
38 Fanatical
41 Tom of "Reuben, Reuben"
42 Grunts, so to speak
43 Send out
44 Hard to see through
45 Sixth-century Chinese dynasty
46 Take the gold
47 Mistletoe feature
48 "... could ___ fat"
49 Sort of
51 City near Glacier Bay National Park
52 "Just wondering"
53 Tops
54 1.101 liters
55 Exactly so

DOWN

1 Opera on which "Rent" is based
2 Rosary prayer
3 Bomb
4 As a companion
5 She played WKRP's Jennifer
6 "What's more ..."
7 Canoeist's maneuver
8 Looks for
9 The Legend of ___: early Nintendo game
10 "The Wizard of Oz" farmhand
11 WWII command
12 Godlike
13 Spent
14 It's elegant when turned
20 Like "Pick a cod, any cod"
23 Bee product
24 Tops

26 Made out
27 Five-alarm item
29 Send
30 Risque
32 Worthless
33 Least burdensome
34 Turn off totally
35 "I give up"
37 Sign in a window
38 Get back to the beginning, in a way

39 Key with no sharps or flats
40 Like 101011, say
41 Blinking light
44 Bright bunch
45 Port of Crete
47 Steady
48 New money
50 Et ___: and the following
51 Petticoat, e.g.: Abbr.

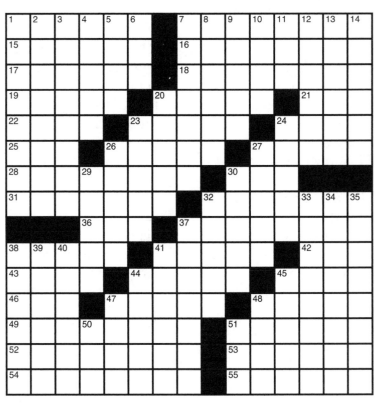

26

BY NORMA F. FRIED

ACROSS

1 Send back to a lower court
7 Mocks
13 Natural habitat
15 Quit
16 Faith-based conflict
17 "The Red House Mystery" author
18 Place for mil. letters
19 Rigorous
21 Florida Congressman Crenshaw
22 Some calls
24 More than please
26 First name in architecture
27 Jumping-off pt.?
28 Most artful
30 Former Vietnamese chief of state Bao ___
31 Legendary Nepalese giants
33 Word of obligation
35 Pres. title
37 Specter, once: Abbr.
39 Rock blasters
40 Inuit in a 1922 film
42 Tom of "Saving Grace" (1985)
44 ER arrival
45 Find

47 Bankrupt carrier of 2001
50 Contests
52 Walker of "Cheyenne"
53 Unleashes
55 Nursery event
57 In readiness
59 Petition
60 Advances beyond usual limits
62 Denounce
64 Talker at the station, maybe
65 Big spreads
66 Multitudes
67 Polite offer

DOWN

1 Recovery project, briefly
2 Joins without much notice?
3 Hall of Fame slugger since 1951
4 "High Noon" heroine
5 Paper contents
6 Genetic court evidence
7 Spanish Mrs.
8 Cook book
9 Suppose
10 Went out of business
11 Grave doings
12 Olympic Games taboo
14 Vine support
15 "The Inferno" author
20 Engage in high jinks
23 Decline
25 Capital of Spain?

29 "___ does it!"

32 Sci. concerned with biomes

34 Overlooks

35 Acquired

36 Scared to the max

38 Inconsiderate

40 Wimp

41 Catholic fraternal org.

43 What you pay

46 Very friendly

48 Not tricked by

49 Sharpness

51 Put up with

54 Vague perception

56 Vigorous

58 ___'acte

61 Knock

63 Calendar box

1	2	3	4	5	6			7	8	9	10	11	12
13						14	■	15					
16							■	17					
18			■	19		20		■	21					
22		■	23	■	24			25	■	26			
■	27			■	28				29	■	30		
■	■	31	32				■	33		34			
■	35	36			■	37	38	■	39				■
40				■	41		42	■	43			■	
44			■	45		46				■	47	48	49
50			51	■	52					■	53			54
55				56	■	57			■	58		59	
60				■	61		■	62		■	63		
64					■	65						
66					■	■	67					

27

BY JAMES E. BUELL

ACROSS

1 Hot item
11 Cook
15 At large
16 ___ fever
17 They have their ups and downs
18 Not supporting
19 Buddy Holly trademark
20 Delicate
22 Florida's ___ City, near Tampa
23 Carousing
24 Explorer Sebastian
27 Small team
29 Proficient
30 Not even close
32 Orchestrate
34 It may be uplifting
35 Reach over
36 Cleaning cloths
38 Fence
39 Quirk
40 Minute opening
41 Loath
43 Linen tape used for trimmings
45 Unmatched
47 Some recesses
48 Bavarian cream ingredient

50 River that forms the Lake of Thun
52 Crops up
53 Missouri River capital
57 Shortstops may apply them
58 It's better when it's smooth
60 Resounding response
61 Minded
62 Coiffures
63 Millionaire's artery?

DOWN

1 Baloney
2 Prefix with dermal
3 Chief attraction
4 Taper
5 Saw-toothed
6 Warrior exiled by Alfonso VI
7 Added topsoil to
8 Red figure
9 Residential suffix
10 What's left, in Le Mans
11 Stretched
12 Steering devices
13 Venture
14 Andersen output
21 Former Indiana senator Bayh
23 Raison d'etre
24 Lambastes
25 Downhill competition
26 Kind of poster
28 Elevated

31 Couple
33 Simile center
37 Monopoly token
38 Habitual criminal
40 "The Mod Squad" role
42 Predatory critter, in dialect
44 Catches, in a way

46 Exquisite
49 Agave fiber
51 Jerks
53 Rock or sea follower
54 It may be hitched
55 Farm shelter
56 Tie
59 Narrow inlet

28

BY BOB PEOPLES

ACROSS

1 Smart answer
10 Cad
15 Beset with misfortune
16 With 64-Across, wavering
17 Succeed during a drill?
18 "Nouvelle Vague" star Alain
19 Male mallard
20 Sorority letters
22 Dada cofounder
23 Bass ending
24 Inclined
27 Cologne trio
28 Korean War fighters
30 Kind of daisy
31 "You Can't Get a Man With ___"
32 Sweat, so to speak
34 Nest noises
36 Old greetings
37 Early form of transportation
38 Spa offering
41 Erosion protection
45 ___ example
46 Pup bearer
48 Stead
49 Train parts
50 Kind of necklace
52 Frequent Peabody Award winner
53 Schubert's "The ___ King"
54 Glance over
55 Make ___ of: botch
57 Top
59 Hopi ritual
62 Astound
63 Really dresses down
64 See 16-Across
65 Goose-bumps feeling

DOWN

1 Proverbs
2 Mass recital
3 Curious
4 Composer Satie
5 Fountain orders
6 Poe's "The Murders in the ___ Morgue"
7 Hosp. classification system
8 Ship built for speed
9 He played Frasier
10 He-men's prides
11 San Jose-to-Modesto dir.
12 Free
13 Fortify
14 Alley game
21 "Well!"
25 Curl worn by 17th-century courtiers
26 Lugs
27 Devilishly intricate

29 Lovers
33 Reproductive cells
35 Hack
37 Fish for
38 Rink confrontation
39 More often than not
40 N.L. career strikeout leader Steve
41 Tolerate
42 It may be poetic
43 Shooter's protection

44 Shooters' subjects
47 Craving
51 Concern of one in the fast lane?
54 Hot under the collar
56 "If He Walked Into My Life" musical
58 One of seven
60 Exasperation
61 Japanese computer giant

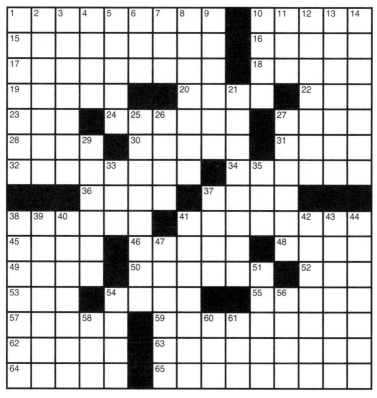

29

ACROSS

1 Michael's ex
10 Wade indelicately
15 Currently
16 Word never used in "The Godfather"
17 Idle and then some
18 Idle and then some
19 Former pullet
20 Headband?
21 Dashes
22 Shades on the beach
23 Worked (up)
24 Eastern ideal
25 Agreement
28 Strikes
30 Cursed
31 Like some suburbs
33 Bodybuilder's pride
34 Philanderer in a Caine film
35 1859 Eliot hero
36 Anti-Union choice
38 Plains drifters
39 Cellulose eater
40 "Please stay!"
41 Holiday buy
42 Fingers
43 Hockey position
44 Discount
46 Revel
47 Ed.'s pile

50 Dizzying designs
51 Exhausted
53 "Mr. Pim Passes By" playwright
54 Blood vessel connected to a capillary
55 Gourd family fruit
56 Embellished

DOWN

1 Lid attachment
2 "___ Jury": 1982 film
3 English
4 Boxer's remark?
5 Marsh hydrocarbon
6 Not on the level
7 Theater supplies
8 Words before many words
9 Sci-fi staples
10 Place of refinement
11 Superman's mother
12 Worth noticing
13 More than just indisposed
14 Actress Signe
21 Contradict
22 Not as involved
23 Corner
25 Vile Nile creatures
26 Hon
27 It's used in some shootouts
28 Friday's creator
29 River sport
31 Venting aids

32 Big name in standup
34 Digression
37 Infatuated
38 Bananas
40 Distributes, with "out"
41 "The Art of Loving" author
43 Fritter away

45 River under the Ponte Vecchio
46 Former congressman Bob
47 Kind of ring or swing
48 Chekov neighbor
49 Part of a flight
51 Gob
52 Conk out

30

BY BOB PEOPLES

ACROSS

1 Reactionary, informally
9 It's always at the end
15 Very busy
16 They have chapters
17 Prig
18 Saw-toothed formation
19 Religious sch.
20 Victor Vasarely's genre
22 Kuklapolitan Players member
23 Records
26 Portuguese explorer Bartolomeu
28 Word with living or dead
29 Episode
30 On the up-and-up
31 "It's ___!": "Yes!"
32 Struck out
34 City with a view of Vesuvius
36 Crown
37 ___ blocker
38 Critical report
41 Hermes's staff, in Greek myth
45 According to
46 Climbing rope material
48 Provoke
49 IBM competitor
50 Efficient type
51 Gnaw
52 Swindle
54 Counter
57 Fancy marble
58 Strike
60 Case part
63 Stable scene
64 Assumed control
65 Genuine
66 1980 Sam Shepard play

DOWN

1 Goon
2 Legally out
3 Nonplussed
4 Sow or cow
5 Actor Kingsley
6 King of old comics
7 Beginning of a house?
8 Massaged
9 Experienced, as losses
10 Prefix with color
11 Feudal estate
12 Actually
13 Reachable
14 Pencil game entries
21 Fix
24 Zhou ___
25 Grant
27 Formal act
30 Barker of "La Dolce Vita"
33 Woody Allen, for one
35 Harness race horse
37 Outlaw
38 Loot

39 Spider-Man nemesis
40 Clears out
41 He knocked out Sullivan in 1892
42 Related to feeling
43 Newscast features
44 Two-time U.S. Open winner
47 Protective shelter
53 Speed ratio
55 Wife, in legalese
56 Grand
59 Antonio's "Evita" role
61 Jack's preceder
62 Fiddle stick

31

BY ROBERT H. WOLFE

ACROSS

1 Decide democratically
10 Pledge site
15 Given up
16 Toted
17 Kook
18 Big name in strings
19 Golden ___
20 "She meant a lot ___"
21 1978 co-Nobelist
22 Sepoy Rebellion figure
23 Go back
24 Strength
28 Liquor flavorings
30 "___ gloom of night ..."
31 Corn lily and crocus
33 EMTs' destinations
34 Informative collection
35 Consequences, figuratively
37 Let back in
40 Musket tip?
41 Model Carol
43 Pluck
44 Music producer Brian
45 Praise highly
47 Church areas
48 John of "Full House"
50 Raise
52 Singer Irene et al.
53 "... think ___ my match"
54 Rip off
58 Leaning
59 Agee's "The Morning Watch," e.g.
61 Tri- plus two
62 Gas turbine fuel
63 Guest of note
64 Vets

DOWN

1 Cry of accomplishment
2 In-way link
3 "High Noon" lawman
4 RR employee
5 Oklahoma city
6 Electricity pioneer
7 Gibson garnishes
8 Like some runs
9 Brink
10 Humbles
11 Miller's salesman
12 They may be registered
13 Come between
14 Rubs in, so to speak
22 Angler's need
23 It's pressed at alleys
24 Apartment feature
25 Positioned (oneself) relatively
26 Boisterous
27 Cook's meas.
29 Three-time NHL MVP
32 Mail-order pioneer
36 Guileful
38 "O! what ___ of looks ...": Shakespeare
39 Security pmt.

42 Disorder
45 Marquee listing
46 Not at all happy
49 Island south of Sicily
51 Alamogordo experiment
53 Chinese leader?
54 Captain's spot
55 Oklahoma native
56 Move noticeably
57 Freshwater delicacies
60 Island chain?

32

BY JAMES E. BUELL

ACROSS

1 Mariner's domain
10 Aquarium acrobats
15 Yet to be developed
16 Baseball's "Little Colonel"
17 Acted panicky
18 Wide open
19 Took in
20 View from Darjeeling
22 Family nickname
23 Until this point
25 Highway cruisers
27 Needle
29 Peace Nobelist of 1994
30 Apply a basecoat to
33 Slightly open
36 Gyro holder
37 Prestigious wheels
38 Reason of "Salome"
39 More miffed
40 "World's number one fashion magazine"
41 Request after a cut
42 Some university dormers?
43 Quarter of a score
45 Partnerships, often
47 Piling up
50 Raised a nap on, as leather
54 Bunk

55 One with a promising future
57 Canton divided by the Reuss River
58 Elicit
60 Go ballistic
62 It's been seen before
63 Wind
64 Road hazard
65 Freezes

DOWN

1 Nursery rhyme name
2 Sister of Euterpe
3 Ivy-covered, e.g.
4 Lower Saxony river
5 Special touches
6 Warded (off)
7 De Valera's land
8 Ward off
9 Exodus commemoration
10 Daniel Webster, for one
11 Gas pump abbr.
12 Pre-peace talks demand
13 Said "Ha!," e.g.
14 Reels from a blow
21 Get really high
24 Commemorative bands
26 Tribe infant
28 Gain
30 Accountants, at times
31 One worth emulating
32 Orneriness
34 Nozzle

35 Canned
39 Ones gathering information
41 Mine entrance
44 Thumbs-up
46 Runs out of
48 Nasal passages
49 Bestow
51 One of the Allman Brothers
52 "An Unmarried Woman" heroine
53 Ate
56 Resort near Venice
59 Preceding line, often
61 Rake

1	2	3	4	5	6	7	8	9		10	11	12	13	14
15										16				
17										18				
19			■	20				21			■	22		
23			24			■	25				26			
■			27			28		■	29					
30	31	32			■	33	34	35		■	36			
37					■	38			■	39				
40				■	41				■	42				
43				44		■		45	46			■		
47					■	48	49	■	50			51	52	53
54		■	55				56			■	57			
58		59		■	60					61				
62				■	63									
64				■	65									

33

BY BOB PEOPLES

ACROSS

1 Disreputable spokesman of the '80s
9 Counterargues
15 Article addenda
16 First name in mystery
17 Fashion industry, slangily
18 Elite decade
19 Fool
20 Doesn't keep from
22 Dwindle
23 Fr. company
24 Also
27 Straight from the horse's mouth?
28 Early discount gas chain
30 Western pickup group
31 Sitcom named for its star
32 Parlor pieces
34 Vacation mementos
36 Defeat
37 Cut with a knife, old-style
38 Skillful
41 Feller in a forest
45 "She's ___ Mama Jama": 1981 hit
46 Sharper
48 "Comin' ___ the Rye"
49 Applies gently
50 Very popular
52 Sun Devils of the Pac-12
53 An ex of Rita
54 Pierre's home: Abbr.
55 Tree with sensitive leaves
57 Cash register key
59 Researcher's asset
62 Stuck
63 War of 1812 battle site
64 1999 "Annie Get Your Gun" star
65 Logs

DOWN

1 Ancient Jordan River city
2 Losing
3 Most uptight
4 Intrigued by
5 A bit, colloquially
6 Hagen of Broadway
7 Letter in the London Times
8 Vain
9 Sidewinder, for one
10 Some are fragile
11 Carter or Clinton: Abbr.
12 Put into words
13 '20s-'30s baseball nickname
14 Gulf of ___: Panama inlet
21 High lines

25 Flakes
26 Policy expert
27 East
29 Pyramids, e.g.
33 Cool amount?
35 Roundish welcome
37 Restaurateur Toots
38 Imbibed modestly
39 Mother-of-pearl source
40 Made some pin money, perhaps

41 Culinary contest final
42 Simpson attorney Robert
43 First name in talk TV
44 Hurt
47 FDA guideline
51 "La Vita Nuova" writer
54 Stain
56 Fish-eating duck
58 It may come after you
60 Luau staple
61 Trip

34

BY ROBERT H. WOLFE

ACROSS

1 Improvised, in a way
8 As a substitute
15 Old hand-to-hand combat weapon
16 Chilean natural resource
17 Kind of priestly veil
18 "The Divorcee" Oscar winner
19 Letter from Corfu
20 When Romeo says, "Juliet is the sun"
22 "O Pioneers!" author Cather
23 Takes off
25 Spanks
26 Choice cut
27 A daughter of Mnemosyne
29 Took a chair facing
32 More than ask
33 Part of a score
35 Words spoken while flexing a finger
37 First class action?
39 Mover
42 Unwelcome watcher
46 1967 NHL Rookie of the Year
47 "... ___ ghost!"
49 Took
50 "Amores" author

52 Cut for an agent
54 Most difficult part
55 Ticketed
57 Union member?
59 Env. contents
60 Of the past
62 State
64 Took
65 Headway
66 Polecats' relatives
67 Some rugs

DOWN

1 Formed into a rounded shape
2 Designer clothes
3 Handy reference
4 Symbol of perfection
5 Skater Lipinski
6 Not about
7 Three-sided formations
8 Demand
9 Govt. research group
10 Fuss
11 Hiker's route
12 Ring site
13 Artist's studio
14 Make nuts
21 Trapped, sort of
24 Old hat
28 Group Theater member of the 1930s
30 Three-time A.L. Gold Glove winner Otis
31 Camp sights
34 Uruguay's Punta del ___

36 Uncultivated tract
38 Gardener's preparations
39 Loaf
40 First name in flight
41 Hard worker
43 Braciola, in France
44 Shade source
45 Stifle

48 Surrounded by
51 Block
53 Start of a poetic dedication
56 They're rolled on tables
58 Light brown
61 Came across
63 Freshness

35

BY KENT LORENTZEN

ACROSS

1 In a memorable way
8 They have pits
15 Twists
16 Repeating
17 Dog used in law enforcement
19 Stuffed
20 Speedy equine
21 Using
22 "Break ___!"
23 Very dry
24 Austin of "Knots Landing"
25 Cartoon dog
26 Support pieces
28 Suppress
29 Stagger
31 Black and others
32 Negotiations preceder, in some cases
34 Greenhouse gadget
37 In these times
41 Co-Nobelist with Menachem
42 Lover
43 Pin site
44 "I Lost It at the Movies" author
45 Put-on
46 Shipping deduction
47 Hunk of history
48 Antony's love?
49 It may be hidden
51 Bygones
54 Stir up
55 Nickels and dimes
56 Did a trainer's job
57 Stockpiled

DOWN

1 Falls between two countries?
2 1983 World Series champs
3 Heavy downpour
4 Lay ___
5 Remain
6 Command
7 Fashion monogram
8 Kind of grove
9 Bothered a lot
10 Balkan War participant
11 Discount label abbr.
12 Artlessness
13 Pro choice
14 Melodic passage
18 Some ceramics
23 Bigmouth, e.g.
24 Dragging
26 Disdainful look
27 Storyteller
28 Packaging material
30 Of base eight
31 Flightless bird
33 Draft feature
34 Fight in a big way
35 Fit to be tied

36 Worry
38 Actress Plummer et al.
39 Montana statistic
40 Fit to be tied
42 Was rude in a crowd, say
45 Whopped, old-style

46 Winter forecast word
48 "I don't give ___!"
49 Smidgen
50 Karmann ___: sports car
52 LAX posting
53 Elvis's record label

36

BY WILLIAM I. JOHNSTON

ACROSS

1 French vocalist nicknamed "The Kid"
5 "If ___ meet ..."
10 Contends
14 "Don't make ___ complicated"
15 Canadian author Alice
16 "Wild Child" singer
17 Creamy desserts
20 Most tight
21 Camel performers
22 Driver's org.
23 Chances, briefly
25 Ohio, for one: Abbr.
26 Die cast?
28 Cool time in Cádiz
30 Esteemed ones
33 Symbiosis
36 Never, in Nuremburg
37 Relief
38 Tee follower
39 Lilt syllable
40 Sympathetic response
44 Feminine ending
45 Three-time Masters winner
46 Prefix meaning "current"
47 Back in the U.S.S.?
49 Fumble
50 20-20, say
51 Respects
54 Lost amount
58 Star of the film "UHF"
60 Holiday decoration site
61 Rate of return
62 Not used
63 Hook hand
64 Bridge call
65 Fascinated by

DOWN

1 Third-century invader in Britain
2 "___ Jury": 1982 film
3 Instead
4 Listed, in a way
5 Old Testament prophet
6 Kept mum
7 Canadian prov.
8 They precede openings
9 Ouse River city
10 Remnant
11 Blissful
12 Wolf, at times
13 Talk back to
18 Jersey hangout
19 1958-61 political org.
24 Get-up-and-go
26 Request to one in a chair?
27 Roll flavoring
28 Gets People in shape
29 Early first-century date
31 Hal of the '70s-'80s Royals
32 It was disbanded 6/30/77

34 Not much hope
35 Article written by Marx?
41 Court arbiter
42 Word for a dam
43 Libya's largest city
48 Actor Danson
50 "___War": Shatner series

51 Cote girls
52 Sewer line?
53 "You didn't say ___"
55 Wraps up
56 Talent
57 Outer: Prefix
59 Pro vote

37

BY BOB PEOPLES

ACROSS

1 Car thief's destination, maybe
9 Online mgrs.
15 Short work
16 Young hen
17 Trouble
18 Symphony that includes a funeral march
19 National rival
20 Because
22 Camper
23 Group with the #1 album "Out of Time"
24 Paving crew members
25 Close
26 Quickly
28 Frozen Wasser
29 1969 Alan Arkin film
30 Semiconductor components
32 Contribute
33 Links holders
37 Tapestry fiber
38 Parts of steps
39 Tennis edge
40 UPS unit
41 "I've seen enough"
45 Like, like
46 Black-plumed bird
48 Snap
49 Four, usually
50 Bemoan
51 Kind of novel
52 Torino locale
54 "Measure for Measure" heroine
56 Destroys
57 Longtime Yankees announcer
58 High-pitched
59 Driving needs

DOWN

1 D preceder
2 President with an engineering degree
3 Not delayed
4 Dogs' dogs
5 Penn, e.g.: Abbr.
6 Click
7 Informal bid
8 Bonnie and Clyde, for example
9 "... Baby One More Time" singer
10 Asian tents
11 ___-pitch
12 1980 Shelley Duvall role
13 Traditional Southern dessert
14 Subs
21 Jobs that involve lifting?
24 Bankroll
27 Suitor
29 "Blue Ribbon" brewing company
31 Wildlife marker

32 Cole Porter's "You Don't Know ___"

33 "Meet Joe Black" actor

34 Coil site

35 Move, in a way

36 Revealing

40 Fold

42 Riding mishaps

43 Lime-flavored cocktail

44 Lots

46 Interrogate

47 "Sometimes a Great Notion" author

51 Take-out order?

53 Test area

55 Cricket club

38

BY RAYMOND HAMEL

ACROSS

1 Leads to
9 Tristram's beloved
15 Highly seasoned white sauce
16 Confining
17 Choke
18 Aardvarks' land
19 Retirement funds
20 They're the lowest
21 Goal for an angry count?
22 Esteemed title
23 Some brews
26 Bug-eyed
33 Ebb
34 Amati relative
35 Single-colored big cat
36 Go cautiously
37 Symbol of strength
38 From square one
39 Take in
40 "Leave It to Beaver" bully
42 Support staff?
43 Public relations employee
45 Abolishes
46 Honk or hoot
47 Phone button letters
49 Pearls' makeup?
53 Cacti with edible fruit
58 British author/radio host Currie
59 Carried too far
60 Steak chef, at times
61 Excited
62 "For shame!"
63 Most melodic

DOWN

1 Play thing
2 Accolade
3 Placid
4 Home movies event
5 Texas A&M player
6 Untapered cigars
7 Kind of collar
8 Wraps (up)
9 Trapped
10 Kenyan adventure
11 Pulls a boner
12 "Armageddon" novelist
13 Mad
14 "... ___ but the wind": Byron
22 Penetrate
23 Pipsqueak
24 Where to get down
25 Aquatic plant life
27 Fuddy-duddy
28 Living
29 Flake
30 Spicy Eastern cuisine
31 Correct
32 Coolidge's vice president

40 Set aside, as for a specific purpose

41 Stand in a corner, maybe

44 Light biscuits

48 TV detective played by Gene Barry

49 ___ Point

50 May 15th, e.g.

51 Lover's acronym

52 Scandal fodder

53 Farm moms

54 Own up to

55 Ridiculed persistently

56 Responsibility

57 Michaelmas mo.

39

BY BOB PEOPLES

ACROSS

1 Places to hear battle stories
9 Spy's break-in, in slang
15 Yells
16 Shooting star?
17 Dependent, usually
18 Boasted
19 One taking a lot of notes
20 Elbow
22 John, for one: Abbr.
23 "___ dreaming?"
24 Make back
26 Like many old records
27 Equal
29 Shuffler's request
30 Spanish cordial
31 Band
34 Person-to-person
36 Bamboozle
37 Bud grain?
38 1954 #1 hit
41 Counter
45 Hold with lines
46 1922 physics Nobelist
48 Repetitive process
49 Energy source
50 Winter Olympics event
53 Happy days
54 Legal scholar's deg.
55 Excellent, slangily
56 Seal on a ring
58 British actress Beatrice
60 Essence
62 Bush's first Treasury secretary
63 Without delay
64 "Toastmaster General" of old comedy
65 Schwinn product

DOWN

1 Part of some old-school movie collections
2 Citizens
3 Creeps
4 Make sound
5 Oxeye relative
6 France's longest river
7 1967 Lemmon/Falk comedy
8 Initial instruction
9 Retreat
10 Frigid finale
11 Garden product word
12 Weapon for Samson
13 Vast
14 Canopy support
21 Decision at home
25 ___ waiting
26 Saint Christopher, for one
28 Do-gooder's goal
32 Complaint to a dairymaid
33 Serious surprise
35 Conceived leader?

37 Fertilizer for lime-deficient soil

38 IHOP order

39 Cold War connection

40 Lots of loot

41 "Aha!"

42 One of about 20,000 law enforcers

43 Content

44 Securely placed

47 Pay back?

51 Ottoman dynasty founder

52 Catchers

55 Lots of loot

57 Snack on the trail

59 Sue Grafton's "___ for Lawless"

61 Article in Le Monde

40

BY HARVEY ESTES

ACROSS

1 Begin
8 Begin, for example
15 Major college football's winningest coach
16 Alternate
17 Calls for
18 Limousine attachments?
19 Singer DiFranco
20 Cameo
22 Expensive carrier
23 Dole's running mate
25 Major music market
26 Cut, old-style
27 In a tough spot
29 Light application
30 Hard to get up
31 "... the world's mine ___": Shakespeare
33 Crème brûlée, for one
35 Ahead
37 Covers for little dogs?
39 One doing clerical work
43 Handles roughly
44 Followers of nus
46 Stick in school
47 "Laugh-In" first name
48 Port on the Bight of Benin
50 Clickers on pads
51 Here, to Henri
52 On the throne
54 Choral syllable
55 Way back when
57 Band aids
59 Enters stealthily
60 Auto designer Maserati
61 Helps, as an unhappy diner
62 Healthful routine

DOWN

1 Address
2 Buff maker
3 Off and on
4 "The Crying Game" actor
5 Common paper nickname
6 Off
7 Put up
8 Orient Express terminus
9 Affects emotionally
10 Speak emotionally
11 Like some hist.
12 He played Captain Davies on "Roots"
13 Type of oil
14 Like a marching band
21 V, maybe
24 Leafstalk
26 Box site
28 Makes an impression
30 Harrison associate
32 Map abbr.
34 30-day mo.
36 Snowflake shapes

37 Lines at the checkout counter?

38 Trips

40 Aristocracy, e.g.

41 Hide

42 Arnold's crime

43 "The Armies of the Night" author

45 One on the way up

48 Walk fast

49 Sound asleep?

52 Tabula ___

53 Sharp flavor

56 "Wow"

58 Agnus ___

41

by Bob Peoples

ACROSS

1 Remarkable thing, with "the"
9 Knack
14 If there's no other way
15 Savage
16 Oil, informally
17 "Momentarily"
18 ___ acid
19 "Seascape" playwright
21 Prefix with cycle
22 ER address
23 Three-time '60s track gold medalist
24 Back-talker
25 Pottery glaze
28 Flushed
29 "Well done!"
30 Arab League founding member
32 Lights into
34 Ilk
35 Wheat, e.g.
36 Some dancing shoes
39 Grill on a terrace, maybe
43 Roman emperor after Galba
44 Fashion letters
46 Big name in circuses?
47 Met with
48 Some Cherokees
50 Treasury Dept. bureau
51 In keeping with
52 Book before Micah
53 Ferrara Renaissance poet
55 Zenith
57 "Never mind"
59 Disproves
60 Operating regularly
61 Delightful areas
62 2000 NFC champs

DOWN

1 Stronghold
2 Plant of the buttercup family
3 Meter site
4 Time or life follower
5 Soybean soup
6 Med. specialty
7 It has a floor and swells
8 Queequeg, e.g.
9 Accomplished
10 Salonga of "Miss Saigon"
11 Killer in a Kesselring play
12 Chip maker
13 Chef's creations
15 Some museum visits
20 Salon staple
23 Appropriately named sandwiches
24 Scold
26 ___ of honor

27 "Only Time" singer
31 Ford's press secretary
33 Country singer ___ Keith
36 Extra
37 Immersed
38 1942 Lloyd C. Douglas novel
40 Discipline

41 Highly stressful situation
42 Rats, so to speak
45 Use for support
49 Bogus
52 Powerful streams
53 Jacques of "Mon Oncle"
54 Razor handle?
56 Hired ___
58 Flavor intensifier

42

BY ROBERT H. WOLFE

ACROSS

1 Admonishment to a shrew
7 Standing loss
10 "___ So Fine": Chiffons hit
13 He played Henry II in "Becket"
14 Tilted
17 "Call me Ishmael," for one
19 Eur. carrier
20 "The Crucible" setting
21 Tease
22 Desire
24 Fair
25 Actor Tamiroff
26 By
28 Some tips
30 "Car Talk" network
32 Plant of the legume family
34 Surfing site
35 Lab growth stimulator
36 Spans
39 Leftovers
40 Bell et al.
41 Butcher's cuts
42 Simpsonian institution?
43 Torino tooth
45 Literary monogram
46 "Quo Vadis?" subject
48 Conv. attendees
50 Common Spanish verb
53 Produce cooperative
54 1990 "L.A. Law" Emmy winner
56 Cool
57 It includes the Office of Protocol
60 Gypsum variety
61 Seniority?
62 1960–61 world chess champion
63 Letters from an old empire
64 Crumble

DOWN

1 Hanger?
2 One way to buy stock
3 Breaks out of jail
4 Prefix with combatant
5 First word in Oregon's motto
6 Actress Rowlands et al.
7 Blows up
8 Sedentary sea floor creatures
9 Slam
10 Looking ashamed
11 Surround
12 WWII weapon
15 Isolated
16 Insider's transgression
18 Steal, slangily
23 Trig ratios
27 Wee worker

29 Catchall abbr.
31 $200 Monopoly props.
32 Dark morning brew
33 Summit
35 Originate
36 Turf
37 Phone parts
38 Motel extra, perhaps
43 Senior member
44 "Essays of ___"

47 Emulate Ebert
49 Longtime Senate first name
51 Slight addition
52 More fitting
53 Second: Abbr.
55 Capital of Manche
58 Belittle
59 Year in which Julius III became pope

43

by Harvey Estes

ACROSS
1 Fall guy
6 Fall guy?
15 Old plane handle
16 With cursory perusal
17 Easy melodies
18 Uncivilized
19 Superior, e.g.
20 It precedes di or da in a Beatles song
21 Archer on the screen
22 Poitiers pal
23 Chiseled
26 Attendance fig., perhaps
27 Attach, in a way
28 Rocket tail?
29 "Song of the South" syllables
31 Long-haired cats
33 Exposed area
37 Turbine component
38 Flier's weapon
39 Panama's locale
42 Sewer's protection
44 Drought-damaged, perhaps
45 Pet name
46 Tribute of a kind
47 Bother
50 Finishing some letters?
52 Is no longer
53 First name in early sitcoms
55 Get along
56 Inexact words
57 Venue for Jim McKay
60 Hardly effusive
61 American Airlines Arena team
62 Inventory
63 Mardi Gras decorations
64 They're often waded through

DOWN
1 Separate
2 Land of the Hittites
3 Addressing
4 Web ___
5 Jr. and sr.
6 Makes no sense
7 Eric Rohmer's "___ of Winter"
8 Simón Bolívar birthplace
9 Gp. disbanded in 1991
10 St. in 2000 election news
11 Not often seen, to Caesar
12 Cat-tails bridge?
13 Checks out the merchandise?
14 Fundamental position
20 Olive genus
23 Took to an island, in a way

24 Relative of com
25 Pushing in
30 European cheese town
32 Cry over spilled milk
34 Operating space
35 Decidedly unapproachable
36 Legwear with a Fauntleroy suit
40 Early man's prefix
41 Emancipate
42 Longs (for)

43 Refine
47 President during the XYZ Affair
48 Credit counterpart
49 "Titanic" statue
51 Volga region resident
54 "Woe ___!"
56 1988 swimming gold medalist Kristin
58 ___ mater
59 Electrical measure
60 Boom source

44

BY BOB PEOPLES

ACROSS

1 Easy money
9 Secret symbols
15 Desert
16 Frank Robinson, once
17 Reagan-era scandal
18 Tangled, as hair
19 Hatcher et al.
20 Harnesses
22 Where to find collars and stays
23 "She's So High" singer Bachman
24 Flags at the finish
25 Series starter?
26 Bibliographer's term
29 Rail fixture: Abbr.
30 By and by
31 Zingers
33 It's typically 80% submerged
35 Decline to sign
36 Contemporary of Rex and Ngaio
37 "The Emperor Jones" star
40 It can help if you turn over
44 "That's ___ haven't heard"
45 Hair ornament
47 Strauss opera
48 Chrysler Building architect William Van ___
49 Author Ambler and others
51 Rhythmic genre
52 Excellent, in slang
53 Put away
54 Campus letter
56 Drink made with curaçao
58 Trojan War hero
60 Requite
61 Get something to go
62 Anise-flavored liqueur
63 Address on an envelope

DOWN

1 Waste slowly, with "away"
2 Gilded
3 Warn, in a way
4 R&B singer Braxton
5 Annoys
6 Tony winner Hagen
7 Literally, "baked"
8 Works with one's hands
9 Stumbles upon
10 Bank offerings
11 Site of many a deal
12 Direct link
13 "The Lion in Winter" queen
14 NHL player
21 Specialty

24 Boiling
25 Communications nickname
27 Hippie happening
28 Furies
32 State on the Gulf of California
34 Judy's "Bells Are Ringing" role
37 Guide
38 Furloughed
39 More muscular

41 Speech problem?
42 Not pro
43 Meals
46 What "we have lost in knowledge": Eliot
50 Insect trill
53 Pudding starch
54 Capone's nemeses
55 It's driven
57 "The Conspiracy Zone" channel
59 Seraglio section

45

BY DAVE AND DIANE
EPPERSON

ACROSS

1 Mr. ___: soft drink brand
5 Tropical evergreen
10 "Yeah, right!"
14 Pearl Mosque site
15 Muscateer?
16 Faction
17 Abusive missive
20 Secrets
21 Fresh
22 "Snapshots" novelist Norma
24 Notched
25 Inflexible, as an agreement
28 Out of concern that
29 Send on an impulse?
30 Start of a Hitchcock film title
32 Agcy. in D.C.'s Federal Triangle
35 "The Mod Squad" role
36 Personal histories
37 First name in lexicography
38 Took the initiative
39 Diametric
40 Outrageous, in slang
41 Seas overseas
43 Romantic evening extension
45 Illinois state flowers
48 Response to "Am not!"
49 More than provocative
51 Breakdown of societal norms
54 "Advance Australia Fair" et al.
56 ___ even keel
57 Receive
58 Harem rooms
59 Insignificant
60 Observers
61 Actress Daly

DOWN

1 Literary sobriquet
2 Borodin's prince
3 Having physical presence, as a business
4 Like block lava
5 1997 Nicolas Cage film
6 Rock blaster?
7 Newspaper columnist Herb
8 Queen ___ lace
9 Strike sites
10 Noted entrepreneurial family
11 Prime time fare
12 Driver's lic., e.g.
13 "Grand Canyon Suite" composer Grofé
18 NBC newsman Roger
19 Violinist Zimbalist

23 Central
25 Place for a pen pal?
26 Foreign friend
27 Seder month
31 Hotel features
33 La ___:
Mexican-American
culture
34 Talk ___
36 Bulletin board messages
37 Mediocre
39 Ragú rival
40 1814 treaty site
42 "The Graduate"
heroine
44 Gives
45 Spite
46 Senseless
47 Bit of catcher's gear
50 High spirits
52 "___ Ordinary Man":
"My Fair Lady" song
53 To be, in ancient Rome
55 ___ Lingus

46

BY JAMES E. BUELL

ACROSS

1 Seer's phrase?
5 Spirit of the '20s?
15 Scoop holder
16 Tank protector
17 View from Catania
18 Conflict-ending symbols
19 Layer
20 Spike's original name
21 Fall bouquet
22 Georgia neighbor
24 Commuting sched. entry
25 They can be embarrassing
26 Hollywood figures
31 Overly
32 Glower?
34 Capital on the Gulf of Guinea
35 Superboy's girlfriend Lana
37 Dresden native
39 Tar source
40 Brilliance
42 Update, as charts
44 Nutritional abbr.
45 Usurers
47 Six-time NBA MVP, familiarly
49 Step
50 Brain areas
51 Ersatz gold leaf
55 Delivery letters
56 Ruffian
57 Up close and personal
59 Showy trinket
60 Jumbled up
61 Muséo offering
62 Lets go
63 Hessian river

DOWN

1 1979 Robby Benson film
2 Greyhound carrier
3 Not functionally
4 Get in order
5 Initiations
6 It may be part of a complex
7 14-Down underling
8 Ad ___
9 Accord
10 Swedish university or city
11 Undergraduate Eng. degree
12 Rubberneck
13 Roman road
14 Costner role
23 Word preceding a birth name
24 Senator Thurmond
26 Noted battlers
27 Former RR regulator
28 Place for ballpark figures

29 Industrial link
30 Mythical fire dweller
33 Some warnings
36 "The ___ from Joe's": Ellington piece
38 Unassisted viewer
41 Kind of dancer
43 Stock word
46 Type of relationship

48 Bob Marley's genre
50 Andean shrubs
51 Auricular
52 Writer Jaffe
53 Stylish Brits of the '60s
54 "Step ___!"
55 "The Power Broker" author Robert
58 This way, or that

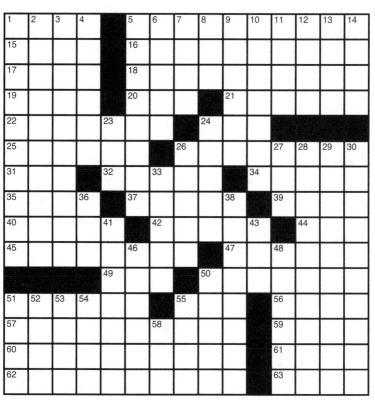

47

BY BOB PEOPLES

ACROSS

1 '70s sitcom high schooler
9 Musical themes
15 Listening device
16 Advertiser's phrase
17 Solo instrument that begins "Rhapsody in Blue"
18 Excite
19 Two-time U.S. Open champ
20 Some anchors
22 Stop: Abbr.
23 Bucks, maybe
25 Sale sign
26 Stud poker?
27 French 101 word
28 Goes blond
29 They have stacks
30 Big name in lawn care
32 Capone associate
33 Ending words of some riddles
36 Lady Jane Grey's crime
38 Teamsters notable
39 Either of two emcees
41 Just for kicks
42 Recognized
43 Confession components
47 ___ call
48 Cunning clerk in "David Copperfield"
49 Incur, as debts
50 Old Testament priest
51 Plant stalk
53 Smoking hazard
54 Pained reactions
56 Caller's need
58 Fanatics
59 Creator of the Mayfair Witches
60 Fight
61 Written rules

DOWN

1 Withdraw formally
2 Father's Day purchase
3 Takeout item?
4 Loan letters
5 Becomes less dense
6 Sharpen
7 Traveler's purchase
8 Prepares
9 Perth pals
10 "Chocolat" actress Lena
11 Hosp. administration?
12 Mills Brothers contemporaries
13 Was strong enough for
14 Does a bailiff's job
21 Fail to understand
24 Like sleep, ideally
26 Type of massage
28 Monk's title
29 Supermodel Sastre
31 "Misery" costar

33 Snowstorm hazard
34 Hickam Air Force Base site
35 Torments
37 Spreadsheet line
40 Tribe allied with the colonists
44 Absorbed, informally

45 Subtlety
46 Binges
48 State bordering Bavaria
49 Find a new tenant for
51 Resound
52 Singer Cantrell
55 Appt. book lines
57 Robert Morse title role

48

BY LYNN LEMPEL

ACROSS

1 Large-scaled fish
7 Road safety maneuver
15 Sweeties
16 Directly
17 Preserved, in a way
18 One dwelling
19 Give up
20 Polly Holliday sitcom
21 "Gandhi" costumes
22 Convinced
23 Projecting part
25 Queen abandoned by Aeneas
26 It may be high-grade
27 Matures
29 Rather good at reporting?
30 Most like suet
32 Catch on
34 Snap
39 Downed
40 Vigorous feelings
41 Calendar abbr.
44 They're on their way up
46 Bag
47 Expanse
49 Abounds
50 Enraptured
51 Jeered
53 Light line

54 Prepare to hit the road
55 Computer accessory
57 "The Merchant of Venice" heroine
58 Assign
59 Get to go straight?
60 Main strength?
61 Name of six English kings

DOWN

1 Struts one's stuff
2 Like older LPs
3 Whole
4 Split, so to speak
5 Example
6 Ship's heading: Abbr.
7 Game with apes
8 Confederations
9 '50s–'60s pop singer Barry
10 Cord components
11 Three-time PGA Championship winner
12 Passionate
13 Iroquois tribe
14 Man or woman
20 Cover, as a cake
23 Ancient Roman magistrate
24 What well-wishers hope for?
27 Aptitudes
28 Bartletts
31 Dedicatory title words
33 H.S. requirement

35 Hostile
36 Flood, say
37 Joining forces
38 Reckless adventure
41 Molten substances
42 Brightly colored bird
43 Space cloud
45 Add sparkle to?

48 Sixth-century B.C. storyteller
50 "Grand Hotel" star
52 Like New York's Chrysler Building
54 Taken off
56 Handle awkwardly
57 Boxer, slangily

49

BY ROBERT H. WOLFE

ACROSS

1 Not straight
10 Caseworkers?: Abbr.
14 Appliance with a magnet
15 "Honour is ___ scutcheon": Shakespeare
16 Law enforcement concern
17 It may be dunked
18 Took off
19 Light opening?
20 Dijon deeds
21 Took in
22 Kind of pleasure
24 Gulf st.
25 They're recommended
26 Nursery song locale
28 Still
31 Glowing, maybe
32 Italian resort city ___ del Garda
33 Appeal
34 Cheer
36 Penultimate storybook word
37 Banned growth-retardant spray
38 People at a kiosk, briefly?
39 Most pleasing
41 Food processor?

43 Big bang creator
44 Old English letter
45 Main drags?
48 Start of a classic trio
51 Deem necessary
53 That, to Pedro
54 Concrete section
55 Had a row
56 Set limits
58 "___ directed"
59 Eschew neutrality
60 Apt. feature
61 Impasse

DOWN

1 Ghana's capital
2 Smart card?
3 Coriander cousin
4 City on Norton Sound
5 Galoot
6 Revelation site
7 Eaten persistently
8 They're usually blue
9 Before, before
10 Big name in snack food
11 Hesitant
12 Sweethearts
13 Earmarks
15 Fred's first partner
20 Bed maker's tool
22 Gun's issue?
23 Beehive State college team
25 "The Wreck of the Mary ___": 1959 film
27 Straight up

28 Widens, as a heading
29 Anxious
30 Belt maker of yore
31 Persian, e.g.
35 Artist Chagall
40 Officeholders
42 Military tactics
46 "Don't Talk to ___ Night": Marc Cohn song

47 City ESE of Kobe
48 Actress Valli of "The Third Man"
49 "Luncheon on the Grass" painter
50 More than large
52 Epinephrine stimulus
54 Like some chances
56 Some rehab symptoms
57 Enzyme suffix

50

BY BOB PEOPLES

ACROSS

1 Hamlet's cousins
6 Indulges in theatrics
15 Keats's "___ Melancholy"
16 Smithsonian collection
17 Victorious Gettysburg general
18 Diner orders
19 Perplexed
20 Families
21 Kit ___ Klub: "Cabaret" setting
22 It may be rare
23 "Shucks"
24 Caesarian section?
25 Like some honored athletes
27 Golfer's choice
28 They get a lot of hits: Abbr.
29 High-muck-a-mucks
30 Operator's request
34 Castle fortification
35 AstroTurf sites
36 Exaggerated
37 "Entertaining Mr. Sloane" playwright
38 Office machine
42 Paradoxical question, in Zen
43 Mail-order record co.
44 Big shot
46 Crimson foe
47 Overplay
48 Texas county in which Paris is the seat
49 Manages somehow
51 Barbecue feature
52 Diamond status
53 Some former winners
54 Memorable
55 Origins

DOWN

1 Sandinista co-founder Borge
2 One-named folk singer
3 Underhanded type
4 Negotiation-ending declaration
5 Surprises, in a way
6 Miscellany
7 Protective charms
8 Threat
9 Caper
10 Jazz musician Zoot
11 Holiday Inn freebie
12 Promoted
13 Straighten out
14 Most ashen
24 Star in Lyra
26 Andes peak ___ Cruces
27 Elite
29 Buck, e.g.
30 Represented
31 One of the Kennedys

104

32 Got to
33 Ford Field player
34 Negotiating team member
36 It's illegal to be on it
38 "Shut up!"
39 Term of affection
40 Author Leonard
41 Bawled (out)
43 Subsidiary of Sears Holdings Corporation
45 Impudence
47 Italian Renaissance family name
50 Type of Internet connection, briefly

51

BY LEONARD WILLIAMS

ACROSS

1 Seat of Clatsop County, Oregon
8 Mold anew
15 Slayers of Harold II
16 Den piece
17 I-80 goes through it in Utah
19 '50s–'60s civil rights activist
20 Geometric fastener
21 Earth, to Caesar
22 Wagons-___: sleeping cars
23 Pitching field
25 Early sixth-century date
26 Daughter of Cadmus, in myth
27 Entertaining clients, maybe
29 Materialize
30 Imitative
32 Springsteen nickname
34 Only
35 Cut out
36 One about to testify
39 Like some professors
43 Kind of bag
44 Irish folklore spirit
46 Actress Brenneman
47 Diminutive suffix
49 Greedy sort
50 It might be foolish
51 Quick as ___
53 Quirk
54 Oscar winner Davis
55 Chinese fruit
58 Poirot portrayer in "Death on the Nile"
59 Trustful
60 Diphthong, e.g.
61 Joins

DOWN

1 Like a sleeping newborn
2 Former "Law & Order" actor
3 Orangutan's nesting place
4 Actor Epps et al.
5 Talks
6 Valuable connections
7 Optionally
8 Truly evil
9 Gate datum: Abbr.
10 Editorial reconsideration
11 Soaked
12 First name in exploring
13 Dodges
14 Requires
18 Beaut
23 Observe unsubtly
24 Bagel topping
27 Bitter
28 "Die Lorelei" poet
31 Peruvian singer Sumac
33 Heat meas.
36 Make mad

37 It's ready for the dryer
38 Erode
40 Xenon, for one
41 Celebrated
42 Tudors, e.g.
45 Scrape, as one's knee
48 Conclude with
50 They're found in lamps
52 Cooper's role in "High Noon"
54 Tick off
56 CD-___
57 Cartoon chihuahua

52

BY JAMES E. BUELL

ACROSS

1 Rackets
5 19th-century riverboat innovation
15 Press in
16 "Rising Sun" actress
17 Yonder
18 Cow
19 "NYPD Blue" actor
21 Prophesied
22 Quenches
23 Sportsmanlike
24 Meant
25 Pittance, slangily
26 Nixon bane
30 Soft foods
31 Gun in a garage
32 Put back in the directory
33 Mom-and-pop gp.
34 Gases up
36 "Talk of the Nation" network
37 Stop surfing?
39 Remiss
40 Corduroy ridge
41 Standing
42 Joule fraction
43 Shrubs with intoxicating leaves
44 Bath cloth
46 Claws
47 Palace occupant
50 Tidal formation
51 Tidy
53 Arrived in time for
54 Revealing
55 Recess refreshment
56 Scales with off-center fulcrums
57 1800s Harper's Weekly cartoonist

DOWN

1 Lump in one's throat
2 Jungle warfare weapon
3 Violent
4 Planks forming a ship's hull
5 Filthy places
6 Can relatives
7 Work on a sub?
8 In an ill-natured manner
9 '20s blues singer Smith
10 Ryan of film and others
11 First, second, or third
12 Withdraw
13 Noted Russian illustrator
14 Bagpipes, for one
20 Spearheaded
23 Military force
25 "Take ___, She's Mine": 1961 play
27 Rum drink
28 Malls
29 Physical part
31 Ring boss

32 T. ___
34 Notwithstanding
35 It's game
38 "The ___ Bridge Club": P.J. Barry play
40 Folklore villain
42 Typos and such
43 Rake

45 Merlin Olsen teammate Grier
46 Numbers
47 Tolkien tree creatures
48 Heart of the matter
49 Evening spread
50 Easygoing
52 Links figure

53

BY BOB PEOPLES

ACROSS

1 It's often depressed
9 Kind of number
15 Center of activity
16 "The Dark Half" director George
17 Haphazardly
18 Trick
19 Fan noise
20 Forensic tool
22 Sites for some organs
24 Squeezes (out)
25 Suffix with proto-
26 Wing
27 Fortified
29 Concert hall
31 Divers' domains
33 "Agnes Grey" author Anne
34 "NFL PrimeTime" airer
35 Swindle
36 Comes up
39 Bought back
43 Office appointments
44 Evening time
45 Poetic preposition
46 Pres. who appointed Earl Warren
47 Artist who worked on Hitchcock's "Spellbound"
48 Complete

50 Screwball
54 Wine choice
55 Two-time British Open winner
56 Hard copy
58 Unexpected delights
59 "I concur"
60 Hans Christian Andersen's birthplace
61 Junkyards, e.g.

DOWN

1 Protected from the elements, in a way
2 Place for a patch
3 Somewhat
4 Mariner's aid
5 Long time
6 Melville's foretopman
7 In a unified way
8 Later film versions
9 Where Van Gogh painted "Sunflowers"
10 Small, agile deer
11 "I ___ my wit's end"
12 Dress showily
13 Settle, as differences
14 Swindle
21 Gateway 2000 founder Waitt
23 Former Tennessee senator Jim
28 Gym set
29 Accustom
30 Finished
32 Cuban bread?

33 Signify
35 Player whose team changed names in 2008
36 Expand
37 "Quiz Show" director
38 Navigable year-round
39 Fall back
40 Copycat
41 Strike-out

42 Strikes out
44 Prestidigitator's prop, perhaps
47 Compact
49 Big name in lawn care
51 Fed
52 Some bowlers
53 Plaster component
57 Video game letters

54

BY RANDOLPH ROSS

ACROSS

1 Opening statement
9 Currant-flavored cordial
15 Uncle Henry's wife
16 Familiarize
17 Arizona offering
18 Hasn't the knack for
19 Generate interest
20 Arrives piecemeal
22 Girl in a 1965 #1 song title
24 Put down
25 First-rate
26 Dwindled
28 Succeed at the Olympics
30 Trucker's vista
34 Senate happening
35 Got sustenance from
36 Gives
37 Formulated
38 Integrity
39 Avignon aunt
40 Military adviser?
41 "___ been fun"
42 Covered up
43 Was over in no time
48 Stone head?
52 Maltese moolah, once
53 Where French lessons are taught
54 Checks out
56 Most sparse
57 Mountain, e.g.
58 Like some winter weather
59 Former Justice Potter et al.

DOWN

1 Leaves
2 Rube
3 Hot time in Argentina
4 "Lisa Bonet ___ basil" (palindrome)
5 Opposite of maj.
6 She debuted in the cartoon "Dizzy Dishes"
7 Dirty look
8 Sent, in a way
9 Overconfident
10 Kazakhstan border sea
11 Math function
12 Schedules, with "for"
13 Suggests
14 Like a smooth riverbed
21 Heartbreaker
23 Tyson rival
27 Taboo
28 Law maker of 1865
29 "Voice of Israel" author
30 Baseball alumni
31 Larcenous
32 One to one, e.g.
33 "Contract with America" name
34 Lintel site
36 Rumsfeld's gp.
38 Doohickeys

40 Babe in films
42 Unplanned
44 Actress Dushku of "Bring It On"
45 ___ lose
46 Spiner of "Star Trek: The Next Generation"

47 Approvals
49 1920s teacher at the Bauhaus
50 Bit of funny business
51 Ramp, perhaps
55 Cat call

55

BY MARK MILHET

ACROSS

1 Yoda of "Star Wars" was one
11 Sally's "Places in the Heart" role
15 Inconveniently
16 Collected
17 Respond to a pep talk
18 Region
19 Orlando-to-Miami dir.
20 Oft-told tales
21 Bank, often
23 Enlist in
24 Kind of bag
25 Not allow to get too close?
28 Laughing ___: kookaburra nickname
29 That is, to Tiberius
30 XL and others
31 Resting place
33 Screen material
34 Tore apart
35 Withhold
36 Gained a lap
37 Simon & Garfunkel classic, with "The"
38 Ad hoc group of yore
39 38-Across gear
41 Classified
42 Previously

43 Nashville attraction, familiarly
44 Fertilizer component
45 Last words?
46 Blue ___
49 Like many fans
50 Item on the prom to-do list
53 Red ___
54 Pâté ingredient
55 Proof word
56 Exam you can't sit through

DOWN

1 Saw points
2 Montréal seasons
3 Promgoer's need
4 Pugilists' gp.
5 Form letter, e.g.
6 Skillful
7 Severe
8 Ocean motion
9 Big bird
10 Went in for
11 Itching cause
12 Try really hard
13 Not the least bit frivolous
14 Warn
22 Peeves
23 Kid
24 Star follower
25 Designs
26 Subject of a Cosmo test, perhaps

27 Going back to square one
28 Kids, in slang
30 A mile a minute
32 Like Easter eggs
34 They're hard to pass
35 Simple craft
37 Influence
38 Palatial entrances
40 Entertain at bedtime, maybe

41 High points
42 Swiftly
43 Really big
45 Landfill emanation
46 Like much early television
47 Skunk River city
48 Plant suffix
51 Spoil
52 Three sheets to the wind

56

BY BOB PEOPLES

ACROSS

1 Flash
5 ___ Arenas, Chile's southernmost city
10 Red container, maybe
14 Load-bearing piece
15 Hollywood pairs
16 Chills
17 Spice Girl Halliwell
18 Saarinen collaborator
19 "___ less than thou owest": Shakespeare
20 Stand for a change
23 "There is ___ in 'team'"
24 B'way posting
25 Behave
34 Where to find fjord explorers: Abbr.
35 Shine
36 Promote
37 Blue hue
38 Shade
39 Prince Charles, for one
40 Was positive
41 Grainy, in a way
42 Jazz singer Jones
43 Extra conditions
46 Shoe part
47 Vitamin no.
48 Makes possible
57 Few and far between
58 Wretched hut
59 Explorer who charmed Kublai Khan
60 Some reds, informally
61 Lieutenant general at Gettysburg
62 It's a turnoff
63 Some tributes
64 Common budget items
65 Sharon's "Cagney & Lacey" costar

DOWN

1 Lively dances
2 "Humph!"
3 Onetime "Gong Show" panelist Jamie
4 Cooperative court figure
5 Making sense of
6 Where Pioneer Day is celebrated
7 1954 Mason role
8 Some feds
9 Some town hall records
10 Reprimand
11 '40s Time film critic
12 Blabbed
13 Stride Rite brand
21 Beyond the norm
22 Eur. title
25 Stole animals
26 "Sorry"
27 "___ mind"
28 With 51-Down, 19th-century inventor
29 "The Flying Dutchman" heroine

30 "Love Me Tender" leading lady Debra
31 Performs, old-style
32 Pretty
33 Precious instrument
44 Figs.
45 Stir
48 Ricelike pasta
49 Not outstanding
50 River to Donegal Bay
51 See 28-Down
52 Flush
53 Exercise target
54 Hot
55 "The Ninth Gate" actress
56 Mechanical method

57

BY SHERRY O. BLACKARD

ACROSS

1 Nobel physicist Rabi
7 Cozy site
13 Painted Desert natives
15 Not natural
16 Royal features
18 Seat, briefly
19 One of the Titans
20 Smashed
21 LAX postings
23 Actress Best et al.
24 Subscriber's bonus, perhaps
25 "___ say ..."
27 Deli request
28 Actor/singer/dancer, in theater lingo
34 Onetime Atl. crosser
35 Part
36 Lummox
39 Morning-after nip
41 "Arabesque" costar
44 Really appreciate
45 Race place
46 Impressive note
51 Work on the floor
52 Oater command
53 Setbacks, slangily
55 Airline to Landvetter
56 Song introduced in the 1938 film "Going Places"

59 Enhanced
60 Golden ager, for one
61 Quagmire
62 "Dust in the Wind" singers

DOWN

1 Probes
2 Reacted to being busted
3 Words of exasperation
4 Patriotic org. since 1890
5 "___ be in England ...": Browning
6 Co-creator of the Silver Ghost
7 No-nos: Var.
8 Slaughter in baseball
9 Dr.'s order?
10 Kind of game
11 Wonder
12 Final recipient
14 Brief plan
15 Brash bird
17 Suffix with Caesar
22 Longtime Richard Petty sponsor
24 You'll have a blast with it
26 City on the Allegheny
27 They may be bleeped
29 Biblical judge
30 Three times, in Rx's
31 Physician's gp.
32 Call a game

33 "The Lord of the Rings" being

36 Cabinet

37 "No running" zone

38 Ways out

39 Scandinavian goddess

40 Put away

41 Mill problem

42 Capital of Asturias

43 Not for most teens

46 Smarts

47 "___ Proud": 1964 Impressions hit

48 Suburban automaker

49 Munich address

50 Alabama native

53 Resting places

54 Biological bristle

57 Princess's problem, in a fairy tale

58 Hat or hair attachment

58

BY JAMES E. BUELL

ACROSS

1 Burns, for instance
5 Cops out
15 Barnstorm
16 Sparing
17 Pretentious
18 Somewhat angelic
19 Supporters
20 January 13th, e.g.
21 Packed
22 Held up
24 Language group to which Lao belongs
26 It's inflatable
27 Claudius I's successor
29 Styling gel
34 English city known for its porcelain
36 Stare
38 Copy machine insert: Abbr.
39 Contest for the well-balanced
42 First Earl of Avon
43 Without assurances
44 Type of question
45 Objective
47 It may involve a keyhole
49 Top rating
50 Insurance subject
52 It's often last
54 Come close to

58 Matching
60 Morph opening
61 Reactor
63 "Mi chiamano Mimi," for one
64 Improves
65 Items found on Glasgow beans?
66 "Agreed!"
67 Dele undoer

DOWN

1 Daily fare
2 List of fixed mistakes
3 Down at the plant
4 Meeting for two
5 Near
6 Breezed through
7 Handle directly
8 Kosher deli offering
9 Protective compartment
10 Gloria Estefan's husband
11 Met draw
12 ___ rain
13 Narrow passage
14 Iditarod vehicle
23 Debut pop album of 1987
25 Parrots
28 Tiffs
30 Underground operator
31 Silk-stocking
32 Seven, for many
33 Breakfast order

35 Sweet cherry
37 ___ majesty
40 Brussels-based gp.
41 Moppet
46 Hannah's husband, in a Woody Allen film
48 Swiss composer Bloch
51 Parade honoree, briefly

53 Accommodates, in a way
54 Cine addition?
55 Bit of news
56 Rat cousin
57 Exile of 1979
59 Intestinal sections
62 ___-Magnon

59

BY BOB PEOPLES

ACROSS

1 Allocates hush money
16 Masters home
17 Magazine perfume ad features
18 It doesn't last
19 Roy Rogers's birth name
20 Electric ___
21 "The Lady from Shanghai" heroine
23 Pie-eyed
26 Sony competitor
29 Ending for equi-
30 Cheat
34 Old office supply
39 Pope called it "dang'rous"
40 Doesn't care for
41 Opinion, as of the law
42 Org. Roald Dahl joined in 1939
43 River through Devon
44 "Bury my heart at Wounded Knee" poet
46 Answer, briefly
50 "Fame" singer
53 Ran like the dickens
56 Hawaiian furniture wood
57 Sleep lab subjects, e.g.
61 They'll do for now
62 Presents a challenge

DOWN

1 Faux pas
2 Cracker-barrel
3 Old oath
4 Calendar pg.
5 Lat. and Lith., once
6 Space-saving term
7 Panasonic subsidiary
8 Very rare
9 Dundee denial
10 Saturn drivers?
11 Located
12 Sponge feature
13 Deep blue
14 Practice enders, often
15 Real estate broker's aid: Abbr.
22 Glacial formations
24 Bounds
25 Blow out
27 Sacks on a base
28 Burning brightly
30 Long
31 Samuel Johnson portraitist John ___
32 On its way
33 It may come before a sum
34 Game-ending word
35 "Once did ___ an ambush ...": Shakespeare
36 Emcee's need
37 V-shaped fortification
38 ___ fixe
44 Wallops
45 Softens, with "down"

47 Go around
48 1998 Pulitzer dramatist Paula
49 Old hat
50 Precious
51 Book before Obadiah
52 All ears

54 Printer's unit
55 Facilitate
57 Pres. during the Berlin Airlift
58 Fed. claim settler
59 Buffy's network
60 Place

60

BY WILLIAM I. JOHNSTON

ACROSS

1 Letters on trucks
10 Affected
15 First NBC Symphony conductor
16 Bygone Toyota model
17 Snaps
19 Author Blyton and others
20 No more than
21 "___ Three Lives"
22 CIA forerunner
23 "... which ___ was irksome to me": "As You Like It"
25 Early Pilgrim family
27 Container weight
29 Stow below
31 Strikers' gp.?
32 Fetch
34 Belafonte classic
36 Fast delivery
38 Musical modernist's building block
40 Luau staple: Var.
42 Extremist
43 Delayed
45 They may be rolled
46 It's barely passing
47 Rapid intake
49 Part of NIH: Abbr.
51 Lay low
53 Big name in luxury
55 Author Rand
58 "I'm ___"
59 Start of an example
61 Bait
63 As bad as they come
66 High-hatter
67 They may follow ones
68 Uncanny
69 Simple shelter

DOWN

1 Fifth-century pope known as "The Great"
2 High times?
3 Galley helper
4 Cold
5 Mary Hartman portrayer Louise
6 Telephone trio
7 Aboriginal Japanese
8 In a ham-handed way
9 Shopper's notes
10 Boston-to-Nantucket dir.
11 Bombastic
12 Warm and cold dessert
13 Manmade desert border
14 Road sign subjects
18 Revolting type
24 Fix up
26 ___ majesty
28 "Ain't She Sweet" composer

30 Hot time for Nancy
32 Sire
33 Ace
35 Leatherworking tools
37 Garden area
39 Product with "Robusto!" flavors
41 County on the Strait of Dover
44 Presupposed
48 ___ all-time low

50 They were conquered in 1521
52 Emperor crowned by Pope John XII
54 Lay to rest
56 WWI battle site
57 Atoll order?
60 It may be wild
62 Coll. course
64 When 30-Down occurs
65 Hornswoggled

61

BY LYNN LEMPEL

ACROSS

1 "Fathers and Sons" novelist
9 Go around
15 Directly
16 Not quite a ringer
17 Samoyeds, e.g.
18 In a sinister fashion
19 Former Tampa Bay manager McRae
20 Glide
22 Worker, perhaps
23 Kind of coffee
25 Show derision
26 American Whig Party cofounder
27 "You can observe a lot just by watchin'" speaker
29 Mad VIPs
30 Picked
31 Judge
33 Rehearsed
35 Barely swim?
37 Small bird's concern
40 Rock
44 Landed
45 Debussy subject
47 Tennis shot
48 Some issues, briefly
49 Total failures
51 Puffed up
52 Vexation
53 Citizen Kane's last word
55 Chocolate treat
56 Heartless fellow?
58 Woo, in a way
60 Set free, as a bird
61 Vibrating musical effects
62 Check beneficiaries
63 Ambitious sorts

DOWN

1 Electronics giant
2 Loosens
3 They're staggering
4 Word with speed or send
5 They may be split
6 Corners
7 It'll get you going
8 Pension plan features
9 Influential member
10 At hand
11 Narrow-bodied fish
12 Test pattern
13 Free
14 Not moved
21 On edge
24 Shifts, maybe
26 Service providers
28 Invited
30 Shouts
32 Attack word
34 Summer hours in N.Y.
36 Handles
37 Overact
38 Simple wind instrument

39 Pressing quality
41 Dish cooked in a pastry shell
42 Where the Napo River flows
43 Backslide
46 Mystery writer ___ B. Parker

49 Sections
50 More definite
53 Go ballistic
54 Patrick's "Ghost" costar
57 Endeavour astronaut Jemison
59 Gettysburg Address mo.

62

BY BOB PEOPLES

ACROSS

1 Interrupted 1968 football broadcast, familiarly
10 Move furtively
15 Pro
16 One-time Pawnee neighbors
17 Communications statement
18 "Luisa Miller" composer
19 Goes in a lot
20 Let up
22 Hamm of soccer
23 "Bus Stop" playwright
24 Tube VIP
26 Solution: Abbr.
27 Prefix with hazard
28 Support, with "for"
29 Castaway's creation
31 Passé court term
33 English blue cheese
34 Diving position
35 Kelp, e.g.
36 They range from 88 to 108 MHz
39 Origin
43 Terribly affected
44 Lake near Inverness
45 Blowup: Abbr.
46 Messenger ___

47 Michael J. Pollard's "Bonnie and Clyde" role
49 Cry at home
50 Old comm. giant
51 Nephew of Cain
52 Daphnis's lover
53 Truman's Missouri birthplace
55 Become discouraged
58 Calendario page
59 Flirtation
60 Jerks
61 Pamper

DOWN

1 Influential group in '60s fashion
2 Heighten
3 Lame excuse
4 Thanks overseas
5 "Concord Sonata" composer
6 Hunk
7 Jackie O's man
8 Annoy
9 Key of Beethoven's "Eroica" symphony
10 Kings, but not aces
11 Mining suffix
12 One way to lie
13 Prefaced
14 1980s–'90s Cincinnati quarterback
21 Like some diets
24 Dismantled
25 House calls?

28 Mammal with poor vision
30 Wings
32 Run-in
33 Stuffing herbs
36 U.S. Cavalry Museum site
37 Its motto is "Oro y Plata"
38 Gondoliers
40 Oiler channel

41 Effective
42 Came down in pellets
44 "Uh-uh!"
48 Forms
49 Bundle
52 Do a gym exercise
54 Sanctuary
56 ___-pitch
57 "Shine a Little Love" gp.

63

BY JIM PAGE

ACROSS

1 Mount Olympus denizen
9 "ER" showing?
15 Waiting in line, for some
16 Game keeper?
17 1862 battle site
18 Irish poet Heaney
19 Shade of green
20 Company whose logo includes a horse
21 Gillis's pal of '50s–'60s TV
22 Terre Haute sch.
23 More relaxed
26 Shorten further, perhaps
29 Prankster
30 British title
33 Start
34 Some dorm rooms
36 Running unit
37 Reason for climbing?
40 Tax-sheltered investment
41 Gourd fruits
42 "Duck Dynasty" airer
43 Some bids
45 Can
46 Turning point
47 Cosby costar
49 Not in so many wds.?

50 Still with us
52 Sinclair rival
54 ___-relief
57 Cones and spheres
59 Turning muscles
61 Parting words
62 Uncle Remus character
63 35.3-cubic-foot measures
64 Parts of spars

DOWN

1 Some weighted calcs.
2 Russo of "Ransom"
3 Singer James
4 Dermal opening
5 Persists
6 Leak
7 Face shape
8 Crash program?
9 ___ in Charlie
10 Big hikes
11 Running ___
12 Shooting aid
13 Rub-___
14 Promontory
22 Opinion
24 Drops
25 Makes accessible, old-style
26 Round ___
27 Madrid month
28 Airplane squadron
31 Tours time
32 Fencing choices
34 Brownish drawing ink

35 Right
38 Genesis son
39 Mop, perhaps
44 One who delivers
46 Sofa mover
48 Swamp plant
50 Grieg's "___ Death"
51 Boor
53 Small marsh bird
54 1899–1902 war participant
55 Ancient Semitic land
56 Ukr. and Lith., once
58 Lead-in for op
60 TV Guide abbr.

64

BY DAVID AINSLIE
MACLEOD

ACROSS

1 Peppered from above
8 Like some pipes
15 Kind of share
16 Livestock feed
17 Legume family plants
18 Blow up
19 Inventeur's notes
20 Six ft., e.g.
22 Ready to draw
23 Costner role
24 Write without credit
26 They can be deadly
27 Skater Babilonia
28 Investigators
30 Summer drink
31 Mote revealers
33 List shortener
35 Last Stuart queen of England
36 Nitwit
37 Perfume maker since 1982
40 Rebukes
44 Trifle
45 "I've been framed!"
47 Exiled Cambodian Lon ___
48 Wickiups
50 Continental currency
51 Game with a casekeeper
52 "And thereby hangs ___": Shakespeare
54 Submit
55 Vital conduit
56 20 Questions category
58 Leave
60 International accord
61 "Toad of Toad Hall" playwright
62 Father's Day purchase
63 Fixed flats, maybe

DOWN

1 Immobilizes, in a way
2 Former Canadian Prime Minister
3 Lures
4 Old Dodge
5 Partisans
6 Hot time in Montréal
7 Sprint from third
8 Fly over the equator?
9 You might give him the business
10 Pacific port
11 Actors Hale Sr. and Jr.
12 Not complete
13 Film in which Ma and Pa Kettle debuted, with "The"
14 Kind of diver
21 Plenty
24 Stone Mountain makeup
25 Place for roses
28 Old Finnish coin

29 Lifted
32 Ovine outburst
34 Bodybuilder's pride
36 Crummy way to feel
37 Red-faced
38 It's nothing new
39 Many movie monsters
40 Tropical tuber
41 Hot

42 ___ 500
43 Didn't go under
46 Lease prohibition
49 Smooth and lustrous
51 Manuscript sheet
53 Marine divers
55 Charitable offerings
57 Put away
59 Abu Dhabi's fed.

65

BY MANNY NOSOWSKY

ACROSS

1 Lines one's pockets, maybe
5 One of its enemies is the snow leopard
15 Calling company
16 "Get up!"
17 Auto buyer's bargain
18 Each, reciprocally
19 Genetic
21 Old-time bandleader Fields
22 401(k) cousin
23 Admires, and then some
25 Popular computer game, with "The"
27 Removed, in a way
29 Irritate
33 It may elicit a call
34 High tune
36 Never
37 Claim to be so
39 Rosencrantz and Guildenstern
41 Red Rose
42 Update, as for an atlas
44 Not previously seen
46 Play with robots
47 As a whole
49 Adores
51 Suspended vehicle, perhaps
53 Alters a contract, in a way
55 Plant
58 Scrape aftermath
60 Prophet who chastised King David
61 Spy wear?
64 "Je te plumerai la ___": "Alouette" lyric
65 Hot
66 Square figure
67 Way to buy flowers
68 Square figure?

DOWN

1 Daughter of Hekzebiah Hawkins
2 Tied
3 Lifelong
4 One may keep you up
5 Rarity for a curmudgeon
6 Spot to crash
7 Votes for
8 ___ Ark
9 Receive, as a radio signal
10 Stage employees
11 Toward the rear
12 Company that became Royal Crown
13 Bucks
14 ___ Plus razor
20 Choice word?
24 Al-Bashir's country
26 "Cut it out!"
28 Drift

30 Comforting words
31 Dreamer
32 Still-life subject
33 Uncovered
35 Seesaw, essentially
38 Poet Whitman
40 Alley challenge
43 Auto pioneer who created the Volkswagen
45 Helen of Troy's mother

48 Hidden
50 Wickerwork material
52 Big
54 "Golf Begins at Forty" author
55 Make the cut?
56 European hub
57 Painful ridge
59 Husband of Ruth
62 High degree
63 Life time

1	2	3	4		5	6	7	8	9	10	11	12	13	14
15					16									
17					18									
19				20			21					22		
23						24		25			26			
	27						28		29			30	31	32
33				34				35		36				
37			38		39				40		41			
42			43		44				45		46			
47				48		49				50				
		51			52		53						54	
55	56	57		58			59		60					
61		62					63			64				
65										66				
67										68				

66

BY MARK DIEHL

ACROSS

1 Preservation aids
10 Building units
15 Is relentlessly antagonistic
16 Dietary label
17 It usually has a lot of fruit
18 Goat god, perhaps
19 The Green Hornet's sidekick
20 Yarn
21 "Who ___ kidding?"
22 Original "Star Trek" studio
24 Relative of nuts
25 Made cutting comments
29 Important fin. yardstick
31 Compassion, initially
32 Texas's state tree
33 "Parsley / Is gharsley" poet
35 Dodger's forte
37 Performer
38 Revolves around
40 One with many parts
41 Discount letters
42 Without feeling
43 Opposite of contrasts
44 Cruising
46 Bud from way back
48 Suffolk sucker

50 Father of Eliphaz
51 Healer
55 No longer a minor
56 Retro style
58 Potpourri piece
59 Drill command
60 Take four of four, say
61 Certain Protestants

DOWN

1 Hide
2 Screen pet
3 It's just an act
4 Sonja Henie's birthplace
5 Ravens' gp.
6 Stunned
7 Met expectations
8 System of gun-barrel grooves
9 "Rikki Don't Lose That Number" group
10 "Kiss me as if it were the last time" speaker
11 Ruling body
12 Lingering sensation
13 He played Poopdeck Pappy in "Popeye" (1980)
14 Handheld transports
22 Challenged the accuracy of
23 ID holder
25 Covert govt. force
26 1959 Sinatra film
27 Words of empathy
28 What was

30 Bring into play
33 Pitch phrase
34 Little chip
36 Double Delight snack
39 "Most likely ..."
43 Olympic wreath
45 Antifouling chemical target

47 Western buds
49 Cry
51 Times Sq. locale
52 Razor brand
53 Describe
54 Become involved (with)
57 Seam find

67

BY BONNIE L. GENTRY

ACROSS
1 Nightclub units
7 Former Senate minority leader
14 Measure of insulating ability
15 Clam
16 Change actors in
17 Scientific series
18 Expunge
19 Twaddle
20 ___ Arc, Arkansas
21 Truth-in-lending nos.
22 Once bitten, so to speak
23 Provoke
24 Official language in Vientiane
25 Big name in whiskey
26 "No man is an island" penner
27 Bookkeeping entry
29 Whopper junior?
30 Spreads rumors
34 Crew member
35 No fluff piece
37 Sacred song
40 Condemn openly
41 Dedicatory title words
42 Main course?
43 Uneven
44 Kisser
45 Ending with law or saw

46 "The Count of Monte Cristo" author
47 University of Western Australia site
48 Adjust, as a recipe
50 Iris covering
51 Unpredictable
52 Like haunted houses
53 Litter components, maybe
54 Alcove

DOWN
1 Quack's offering
2 Like some resented employees
3 Elbows on the table?
4 Designer born in Fort Wayne
5 York's river
6 6–4 or 6–2, e.g.
7 Deprive of heaters?
8 Accord
9 Vague amount
10 Year in the reign of St. Pius I
11 Confrontational
12 Spaghetti relative
13 Maroon
15 Controversial neurosis treatment
19 1990s Israeli prime minister
22 Carafe, often
23 Dick Grayson's alter ego
25 Drummer's cymbal

26 Rapper P. ___
28 Name on a bottle of Spellbound perfume
29 Ride with cars, perhaps
31 Maligned writers
32 One no longer overseas
33 Ballroom dances
36 Walks confidently
37 International labor celebration
38 Bullfight cheer

39 Old Toyota
40 Voices an objection
43 One charged by a judge
44 "Life: A User's Manual" author Georges
46 Spoil, with "on"
47 Sweater unit?
49 Start to use
50 "Suzie Q" band, for short

68

BY DOUG PETERSON

ACROSS

1 Philosophers' fodder
10 Dance at a bar
15 Reserve
16 Fantasyland, e.g.
17 Day time
18 Spine line
19 Rang
20 Subj. of the 1991 film "For the Boys"
22 Big name in Italian coach building
23 Author Bagnold et al.
24 False start?
26 Religious leader Lee
27 Retreats
28 Asked
30 Mary Quant design
31 Blue
32 "The Blue Dahlia" screenwriter
37 British stage actress Staunton
38 Out of sight
39 Picnic loads
41 Roles, idiomatically
45 They may work on drips
46 1937 #1 hit for Tommy Dorsey
47 It's nothing new
48 Lyrically written
50 Calendar abbr.
51 Listing in the Messier catalog
52 "In the icy ___ night!": Poe
54 Conferred
56 Act the villain
57 Walk
58 Minute
59 Contract provision

DOWN

1 Changed the pitch of
2 Sharpen
3 Come by
4 Caves
5 Plot divisions
6 Tear
7 "Another Green World" composer
8 They may be picked
9 Dojo bigwig
10 Smashed
11 "Yeah, man!"
12 Model airplane fuel, primarily
13 Singaraja natives
14 Ornamental shrub
21 Has a larger force than
24 Remain unsettled
25 Moon of Saturn
28 They're suspended at parties
29 Old Western fort
30 Surfing tool
32 Hearty cut
33 Trout ___

34 "Yer darn tootin'!"
35 Jan. honoree
36 Argument weakness
40 Frozen confection
41 Lewis and Clark County seat
42 Turkish mount
43 Oscar night sight

44 '90s host of "The Late Late Show"
47 Tangle
49 "Barton Fink" director
51 Explorer Vasco da ___
53 Cook, in a way
55 ___ cit.

69

BY BOB PEOPLES

ACROSS

1 Long-suffering sports group
8 Spoils
15 Kind of farming
16 '60s Secretary of Agriculture Freeman
17 Cosmetic enhancement
18 Scrap
19 Big hole
20 Suffuses
22 1996 Gore debater
23 Like some Keats works
25 Close
26 Charge
27 Close to an hour
29 You may see them at the source of a traffic jam
31 ___ Bator
32 Electronic music pioneer Varèse
34 Bar serving
36 Endangered ecosystem
38 Freeze order
41 Belonging to
45 Spanish model Sastre
46 Takes excessively, as pills
48 Byzantine emperor known as "The Wise"
49 His, to Henri

50 Zeroes
52 Very wide, at the bootery
53 Express displeasure
55 Slowly realizes
57 MLB statistic
58 The Danube flows along its southern border
60 Buyer's bottom line
62 Done
63 Like the least risky bonds
64 Nautical access
65 Takes steps

DOWN

1 Cooked fruit dessert
2 Solo
3 Topping
4 Media monitoring gp.
5 Burnoose wearer
6 Charles and others
7 Floral enclosure
8 Hustler
9 Stowe's "The Pearl of ___ Island"
10 Stowe girl
11 Fall
12 Certain sickout
13 Like some sausage
14 Increases in intensity, as a storm
21 Comeuppance, figuratively
24 Works together
28 Gift tag word

30 Trickle
31 In jail, say
33 Fall
35 True
37 Frequent caller?
38 Counter cleaner
39 The tiniest bit
40 "WKRP in Cincinnati" news director Les ___
42 Initial advantage

43 Quarterback
44 Cinco de Mayo events
47 Points of view
51 Hägar's hound
54 Finked
55 1962 Johnny Mathis hit
56 Recipe direction
59 Just out of the box
61 Union contract no.

70

BY VICTOR FLEMING

ACROSS

1 Type of heat
10 Acts out
15 Mac source
16 Santa ___
17 Perdita or Pongo of film
18 Daughter of David
19 LAX info
20 Request for a hand
22 Dreyfus defender
23 Lyricists, notably
25 Absorption process
27 Ages
28 Where the law was first observed?
29 End of a rural wake-up call?
30 Sticks
31 Fact
32 Apprentice, for one
35 Mag mogul
38 They're skilled at saving
39 Popular wine brand
41 City for which a Manhattan district was named
42 Globs
44 Pity
45 Hubble's law subject
47 Canapé topping
48 Medicine Nobelist Severo ___

50 ×
52 Book keeper
53 Left one's mark on
54 Annual cultural commemoration
55 Tapes

DOWN

1 Justice Ruth ___ Ginsburg
2 Inability to be moved
3 Spread out
4 Spreading tree
5 Save the day
6 Erie's minor league hockey team
7 Seed coverings
8 Cut the crop
9 Cubs' leader
10 Pinning surface
11 Really focused, slangily
12 Brunch cocktails
13 Inclusive term
14 Author Paretsky and others
21 City near Gelsenkirchen
24 Memorable Nixon host of 1972
26 It launched in 1986
28 Leaves town, maybe
30 Like movies
31 "Holberg Suite" composer
32 Didn't like one bit
33 Helmet opening
34 Tie term, in sports

35 Papal court
36 Wing
37 Potter, perhaps?
38 Lacking tact
39 Some shorts
40 Orbital point

41 ___ Perot
42 Mutes, as piano strings
43 Excites
46 Pizarro founded it
49 Togo's cont.
51 Retired flier

71

BY LYNN LEMPEL

ACROSS

1 Nice thing to hear if you're broke
8 Low-risk move
15 Grime fighter
16 Socko
17 Got results
18 Ridicule
19 Pope work
20 Falls on a border
22 Disco guy on "The Simpsons"
23 Former Canadian statesman Lévesque
25 Battery terminal
26 Fuss
27 Time pieces?
29 In addition
30 Martin of Hollywood
31 Reason to be blessed
33 Was indecisive
35 Hibernation
37 Joiner
40 Embraces
44 1988 Olympics host
45 Official lang. of Fiji
47 Carroll critter that "always looks grave at a pun"
48 Blow
49 Hot pursuit?
51 Literary moniker
52 Accident letters
53 "The Horse and His Boy" author
55 Pond breeder
56 Taboo
58 Authorize
60 Bullies
61 Race figure
62 Makes beloved
63 School basics

DOWN

1 Many wines
2 Partial payment of a kind
3 Computer ___
4 Bygone
5 Nighttime lure
6 Family group
7 Terrible one?
8 Cruet contents
9 With it
10 U.S. disaster group
11 Sight for seer eyes
12 Fan
13 Eliciting feeling
14 Secure at work
21 Smarts
24 Got with difficulty
26 It's a start
28 Longtime conductor of the Cleveland Orchestra
30 Discards
32 Sargasso Sea spawner
34 It's in the bag
36 Unrivaled

37 Soul
38 Beginning of a waxing
39 Honored, in a way
41 Artist's need
42 Frivolous type
43 Renoir's "___ in the Bois de Boulogne"
46 Noted 19th-century advice

49 He played Santa in "Elf"
50 I, sequentially
53 Caesar ally
54 Main attraction
57 Eminem collaborator, for short
59 High dudgeon

72

BY STELLA DAILY &
BRUCE VENZKE

ACROSS

1 They're often framed
16 Gas, for one
17 Moving
18 Lab svc.
19 Trypanosomiasis transmitters
20 Org. in 1974 news
21 Bear's cry
23 Racehorse buyer's concern
24 Part of N/A
28 Below C level?
31 Crocodile Dundee in Manhattan, say
38 So as to ruffle some feathers
39 Emulate a diva?
40 Sale sign word
41 Judicious
42 Wild (over)
45 Pricing spec
49 An ex of Artie and Frank
50 Lack of inhibition
57 GI chow in Desert Storm
58 System fighters
61 Prepare for a premiere, maybe
62 Relaxed to the max

DOWN

1 Chips, at times
2 "Laugh-In" regular
3 Ever
4 Hound
5 Once, once
6 Finders' needs
7 ___-et-Vilaine (French department)
8 Pluto chaser?
9 Scout sets
10 Guelph successor of old Italy
11 Wear the disguise of
12 Bad place to be stuck
13 Pension law acronym
14 Bacterium used in cloning
15 Foreign law body
22 It replaced Milan's Royal Ducal Theatre
23 Aid recipient
25 Cell, maybe
26 Landscaping elements
27 Jones's cocreator
28 Unloading places
29 "It's not my cup ___"
30 Due (to)
31 Go figure?
32 Word of annoyance
33 Dogma
34 Asian occasion
35 Letters before F?
36 Jeff Lynne's rock gp.
37 Rembrandt van ___
42 Italy's largest lake

43 Says without hesitation
44 Auction accessory
46 ___ resin (adhesive)
47 Algonquian speakers
48 "Demian" author
50 What's more
51 Negotiation hurdles

52 Stub ___
53 Silents star Naldi
54 Homer's output
55 Draftable
56 Da ___, Vietnam
59 Baja bear
60 Madeira, por ejemplo

73

BY BRUCE VENZKE &
STELLA DAILY

ACROSS

1 Cut (off)
4 Deadly African biter
9 Span. titles
13 Eponymous British virologist Y.M.
14 Pub request, with "the"
15 Go-___
16 Balance sheet item
19 Certain worshiper's risk
20 Green prefix
21 Olympic skier Tommy
22 Broad-based broadcasts, briefly
25 Marxist article?
28 Freshness
32 Be especially savory
37 1924 novel that won the James Tait Black Memorial Prize for fiction
38 Breaking up
39 Blood type, briefly
40 Eagle or hawk follower
41 Bladed tools
42 Unlike the OED
45 François's friend
47 Ecuador's Cotopaxi et al.
56 Knockout punch
57 They may be kept on suspects
58 Perfume component
59 Putsch
60 Thin strip
61 Outperforms
62 Dean's deg.

DOWN

1 Spike
2 Deep-sea killer
3 Openly won't tolerate
4 "Lives of Girls and Women" author Alice
5 Regarding
6 Tousle
7 Pres. Clinton, for one
8 Morning surprise, often
9 Pushes one's luck
10 1944 Nobel physicist Isidor
11 1968 self-titled folk album
12 Weapon featured in "Exodus"
13 "Nuts!"
17 Market bars, for short?
18 Ming of the NBA
22 "Gabriela, Clove and Cinnamon" author
23 "Fast Food My Way" chef Jacques
24 Unimpressed
25 Herd orphan
26 Traitor, e.g.
27 Fasten anew

29 Broadcast component
30 "Fear Street" series author
31 Some carpets
33 Newsstand item: Abbr.
34 "If I Ruled the World" rapper
35 Madrid's Puerta del ___
36 Woody's ex
43 Brief letters?
44 Place to get clean
45 Great servers
46 Deface

47 Healing ___
48 Beehive oven input
49 Euphonium relative
50 Choice
51 Pops on a diamond, usually
52 Would-be atty.'s hurdle
53 "Preserve me, ___": Psalms
54 Barak of Israel
55 1985 Union Carbide acquisition

74

BY ROBERT MACKEY

ACROSS

1 Host's activity
7 Sprint Cup org.
13 Musical with the song "There Is Life Outside Your Apartment"
15 "Give me an example!"
16 2003 Aaliyah hit
17 One after another
18 Hedonistic constructs
19 Chihuahua time-outs
21 Online "That's funny!"
22 Exigency
24 It might get stuck on a window
25 Factor opening
26 "The Smartest Guys in the Room" subject
28 Zip
29 "Now you ___ ..."
30 Some student aid, e.g.
33 No effort
34 Squeezed (out)
35 Club requirement, perhaps
42 Ariadne's father
43 Model Carangi
44 Twisting and turning
45 City captured by the Allies during Operation Torch, 1942

46 Acting strangely, in rap slang
48 Cultivated
49 King or queen
50 Taskmaster's demand
52 U.N. workers agency
53 Turkish travel shelters
55 '80s Screen Actors Guild president
57 "Chicago" Oscar nominee
58 Word processor command
59 "I would I had any drum of the ___": Shakespeare
60 Rode

DOWN

1 Dearths
2 Easy to see
3 Mosaic piece
4 November victors
5 Van ___, California
6 Earthlike shape
7 South African province KwaZulu-___
8 Latin 101 word
9 Dry, as wine
10 Irish lass
11 Negatively charged
12 Abundantly supplied (with)
14 Aristocratic standard
15 Outspoken Dixie Chicks singer
20 H.S. courses

23 Acted maternally toward

25 Upholstery adornment

27 Creeps up on

29 British guns

31 "___ said before ..."

32 Runner on a slope

35 Company whose ads featured Catherine Zeta-Jones

36 Electrical worker

37 Out for dinner, maybe

38 "Braveheart" garb

39 Mooring areas

40 Luau staple: Var.

41 1972 Bee Gees hit

46 Small amounts

47 Acknowledge tacitly

50 Offer resistance to

51 Swell

54 Edge

56 One of seven

75

BY JAMES E. BUELL

ACROSS

1 Chevrolet Chevelle SS, for one
10 Key of Chopin's Polonaise, opus 53
15 Active
16 Forklift burden
17 Cells don't have them
18 One with dreads?
19 Squeeze
20 Sorry sort
22 Cambodian capital
24 Copy
25 College near Charlotte
29 List on a legal pad, perhaps
30 Fatuous
31 Mâcon's river
33 Vegas beginner
34 They rest on pads
35 Made out
36 Bygone Detroit styling features
37 "___ Man": '60s hit
38 Explorer Vasco ___ de Balboa
39 Smart response
40 Hydrated sodium carbonate
42 Many local volunteers
44 Former Romanian president

46 Eat
47 Metalworker's joint
49 Pull up stakes
53 "Iceland" star
54 Victoria's Secret offerings
56 Russian skater Sokolova
57 Singer in old Muriel Cigars ads
58 ___-O-Matic: sports game manufacturer
59 '90s runner

DOWN

1 Fashion
2 System developed at Bell Laboratories
3 Sports figure
4 Pool room emanation
5 Allow to continue uninterrupted
6 Gets carried away, in a way
7 Pen pal?
8 Maintain
9 Start over
10 Plot
11 Tours site
12 Most recent box office arrival, probably
13 Who's there
14 Quells, as rioters
21 Escapade
23 "___ It": Tom Cruise film
25 Goes down

154

26 Fur
27 One taking off, maybe
28 '60s activists ___'s Raiders
32 Exuded
35 Jerk
36 Architectural guideline
38 "Piece of cake"
39 Autumn apple

41 Layered eye part
43 Straightens (up)
45 Not a good gut feeling?
48 Woodworking groove
50 Withdrawn Uniroyal product
51 Words from the boss
52 Attention getter
55 Fire starter?

76

BY JOY M. ANDREWS

ACROSS

1 Crack, as old paint
10 "Daisy Miller" author
15 Break in the action
16 Mesopotamian, now
17 Evidence of dinnertime expansion
18 Mariner's first destination
19 Acquire a patina, say
20 Old sock feature
21 They may be seen on saddle horns
22 Annual groundbreaker
24 Nicely dressed (up)
26 One of Hack Wilson's record-setting 191 in 1930
27 They aren't good looking
29 Debugging item?
30 Corduroy ridge
31 Goofs
33 Dipteron destroyer
35 Front money?
37 The English one has yellow flowers
40 Makes a flight connection?
44 Sommelier's category
45 Nothing heard at the Louvre
47 Like Bond
48 Not covered by an HMO, probably
49 Cato's appellation, with "the"
51 Gillette's ___ II
52 Queen toppers
54 The old you
56 Tallahassee sch.
57 2001 bankruptcy filer
58 Plea for equity
60 "Funeral Blues" poet
61 All ears
62 Tangled
63 Sycophantic response

DOWN

1 Like a good script
2 Major player?
3 Office gadget
4 Abbr. on a cruise itinerary
5 Turned right
6 Key of two Schubert impromptus
7 It's attached to the steering knuckle
8 Its capital was Bloemfontein
9 Foul caller
10 Danced in a lively way
11 Bay ___
12 Femme fatale
13 Temperate
14 More like a pantywaist
21 Do another draft
23 "Double Concerto" composer

156

25 Subdue
28 Shiner
30 Excuse, perhaps
32 São Miguel is the largest of them
34 They're close
36 Speller's words
37 Lions, Tigers, or Bears
38 Attendants
39 They may be worn with clips
41 Layered dessert
42 Anything but straightforward

43 Seat belt, e.g.
46 What the second of three zeros might mean
49 Shrewd
50 Composer of the song cycle "Evidence of Things Not Seen"
53 Small deer
55 Sen. McCain's alma mater
58 Morgan le ___, half-sister of King Arthur
59 Mil. posts

77

BY LYNN LEMPEL

ACROSS

1 War movie effect
8 Canopies
15 Primary component in nail polish remover
16 Moderate
17 Discombobulate
19 Makes waves, perhaps
20 Silent screen star
21 Means to enlightenment
22 Sale stipulation
23 Hurled weapons
24 Fr. governess's address
25 Trick
26 Winning the lottery, say
27 Has a hunch
28 They may have proposals
30 Uses a hazel tree branch, maybe
31 Diminishing returns
32 Get knocked out
33 Wallops
36 Place to pick vegetables
40 Are unable to stand
41 Be relevant
42 Before, poetically
43 Oscar nominee for "The Godfather"
44 Honeybunch
45 Computer ___

46 One may stand near a curb
47 Collector's item
48 Really cold
49 Regardless
52 Windflower
53 Blog content
54 Lowers
55 Couches

DOWN

1 Old Vegas clique
2 Truman's secretary of state
3 Pâté dish
4 They form many bonds
5 Hauls
6 "Wheel of Fortune" request
7 "___ Until Dawn": 2005 bestseller
8 Ancient markets
9 Cover-ups
10 See 36-Down
11 First name in tyranny
12 Gets affectionate
13 Graceful antelope
14 Cunning
18 Addresses
23 Bring good to
24 Acted hungry, in a way
26 Bygone baseball card brand
27 Venture
29 Singer John
30 Lulu

158

32 Watering holes, so to speak

33 Colin Powell drove it at the 2005 Indy 500

34 Mollusk with an iridescent shell

35 Feigned

36 1982 newcomer to 10-Down

37 Straightest route

38 Organize

39 Make amends for

41 Lofty shelters

44 One of the Allman Brothers

45 For the record books

47 Swift reptile

48 Note passer's signal

50 It appears on the Australian coat of arms

51 Bemoan

78

BY BOB PEOPLES

ACROSS

1 "Our goose is cooked!"
10 City with a California State campus
15 Alpine phenomenon
16 Treatment center goal
17 Fought
18 Uneven
19 FDR predecessor
20 ___ avail
21 Natty Bumppo's creator
22 Nice approvals
24 Stages
26 Angular joint
27 Disgusted
29 Some hyphenated figs.
30 He played Tony on "NYPD Blue"
31 Ineffective
33 Oversimplify
35 Slant found in paper clips?
37 Out of sight
40 Like the sole of a Desert Boot
44 Order
45 Batting practice area
47 Graff of "Mr. Belvedere"
48 Text-interpreting technology, briefly
49 Show up

51 RR stops
52 Hand off again, as a baton
54 Nutritional stds.
56 Magic gp.
57 Stop burning
58 Start of an eyewitness account
60 Cybermemo
61 Bar line
62 Hymn part
63 Austerity

DOWN

1 Use a hose on
2 One taken out
3 TV theme song sung by Frankie Laine
4 She, in São Paulo
5 Rice attribute
6 Leading
7 Blackberry, in botany
8 Eyeballs venomously
9 Reds manager Sparky Anderson's number
10 Eurydice's husband
11 Decorated veteran, e.g.
12 Upbeat words
13 Basis of stare decisis
14 School with the U.S.'s oldest continuously operating music conservatory
21 Enormous
23 Turn in
25 Slight

28 Responded in court
30 Pacers and Rangers
32 Official orders
34 Adriatic seaport
36 ___ the finish
37 Head scratcher's words
38 "Well done"
39 Piece of Pequod gear
41 It may be said during baby talk
42 Permits
43 Makes safe for drinking, as water
46 Salad vegetable
49 Michaelmas daisy
50 Risk taker
53 Pilot starter
55 In stitches
58 Sighs of relief
59 Many yrs.

79

BY KAREN M. TRACEY

ACROSS

1 Color over
6 Diana's escort
10 Stir
14 Cutter cousin
15 Ltr. carriers
16 Uma's role in "The Producers"
17 Corrupting influence
18 Some TV screens
19 Fiber spec units
20 Service station convenience
23 Chero-Cola Company's successor
24 1571 battle site where Cervantes lost the use of his left hand
25 Scottish shaver
28 Mubarak was his vice president
29 Awestruck
31 Place to stick things
35 Inauguration feature
36 Base lines
38 Prefix with -cyte
39 Attack from above
41 Ancestors
43 Lowest card in klaberjass
45 Press kit, e.g.
46 Latin assent
49 Indiana political name
50 Northeastern U.S. highway conveniences
55 Bull: Prefix
56 Via, old-style
57 As a friend, to a Frenchman
58 Athlete married to baseball's Garciaparra
59 Sign of a pen problem?
60 ___ self-defense
61 Smirnoff alternative
62 Child support?
63 Brings down

DOWN

1 Part of a prospective bride's pile
2 Literary pen name
3 Small boat
4 "That's supposed to scare me?"
5 "A Cellarful of Noise" autobiographer Brian
6 Indian territory
7 Hardly ever
8 Movie lover's equipment
9 Sent out
10 Go for it
11 Get straight
12 ___ ease
13 Catch on the range
21 Walking papers
22 Movie-rating org.
25 Wall St. deals
26 What there oughta be

27 Inflict on
28 Henry I of Germany, e.g.
30 Like some mints
32 Tree of the verbena family
33 Nagy of Hungary
34 Outlay
37 Floral leaf
40 Clinks
42 Dried bouquet garni item
44 ___ 1: first manned space mission carrying Yuri Gagarin

46 Revolutionary hero Warner et al.
47 "The Compleat Angler" author Walton
48 Like whitecaps
49 Blighter
51 Alençon's department
52 Kind of debt: Abbr.
53 ___ Ludwig, biographer of Stalin, Napoleon, Goethe, and others
54 Wrongdoing

80

BY ROBERT H. WOLFE

ACROSS

1 1935 Gable/Harlow adventure
10 Soul
15 Watched out for, say
17 Climactic move, often
18 Downhill
19 Salon service
20 Some Thai
21 Yahoo
23 Give out
26 Any ship
29 It often represents time
32 Mickey and others
33 Bears strategy
35 Nothing
36 Sound opening
38 Indian tomb site
39 Big name in fashion
41 The Eagles' "___ Eyes"
42 Hardly patient
44 Elaborate invention
45 Tore
46 Some Harvard degs.
47 Feeds in a pen
49 Senegal's capital?
50 Stumblebum
52 Pro ___
54 "Tasty"
55 "Yes!"
58 Gets ready to chat

62 It may be subject to subsequent spin
66 Be submissive
67 Mythical Himalayans
68 National park employees

DOWN

1 Plastered item
2 "The Farmer in the Dell" syllables
3 Preludes to a kiss
4 More raw
5 Cheerios' cousins
6 Boating hazard
7 Official lang. of Fiji
8 Flurries
9 Sensible
10 U.N. ambassador under JFK
11 Utmost
12 It has a slant
13 Varied assortments
14 Accessory
16 Second in a series
22 Raises
24 Laura Bush's alma mater
25 1980s New York City Opera director
26 Healthful hangouts
27 House player
28 College statistic
30 Apotheosis
31 Hearty, to an old captain
34 Direction to go slow

37 Afterthoughts
40 Some Annapurna climbers
43 General with good taste?
48 Long-legged waders
50 1959 Merman vehicle
51 Folded food
53 One taking cuts

56 Shoe site
57 Year in Caesar's reign
59 Cut, old-style
60 Bakery artist
61 Cape
63 Word with jump or lift
64 Map abbrs.
65 Chemin de ___

81

BY ROBERT MACKEY

ACROSS

1 Evaded security
10 Requests for attention
15 Make certain wedding arrangements
16 Tighten, perhaps
17 Bar brand since 1879
18 Blood groups?
19 Keeps in
20 Author Sewell
21 Austrian soprano Dernesch
22 Black ___
24 Re, to chemists
26 Some bands
30 Words from one who doesn't call?
31 Vitals
33 They hold balls
34 Navel phenomenon
35 Calypso derivative
39 Excavating machine
41 "___ Mater": Latin hymn
45 Not inclined to speak
46 Cage with a son named Kal-el
48 Cheer
49 Conductor Doráti
50 Sounds of uncertainty
54 Mars: Pref.

55 Question about Biblical betrayal
56 Subject of a 1973 Gore Vidal novel
58 Sea wall relative
59 Jack Benny's nemesis in a '30s–'40s radio "feud"
60 Transports using runners
61 Messengers' rides

DOWN

1 Manifest subject
2 Pretend to be what one isn't
3 Castle's portcullis, often
4 Keeps trying
5 Be worthwhile
6 Couturier Schiaparelli
7 "Abraham, Martin and John" singer
8 Model who attended Nairobi University
9 Stock phrase
10 Its practitioners take plenty of bows
11 Capital that's home to the Pioneer League's Brewers
12 Latin catchall
13 Immortal jazz bassist Charlie
14 Bun flavoring
23 It has a seat: Abbr.
25 Premium, briefly
27 "This ___ see!"

28 Mötley ___
29 Solo instrument in "Norwegian Wood"
32 "Procrastination is the thief of ___": Young
35 Warm and friendly
36 Reject
37 Eye-pleasing, as a wall hanging
38 Brass instruments
39 Goes briskly (forth)

40 Finger-pointing word
41 Escargots
42 Fir coat?
43 Unlike a couch potato
44 Went up the river
47 Ray
51 Rhine feeder
52 Charles II's royal architect
53 Covers, as a lawn
57 Abduction suffix

82

BY ARLAN & LINDA
BUSHMAN

ACROSS
1 Perk up?
11 Spellbound
15 Annual spectacle that is never held on Sunday
16 Suffix with decor
17 Like some tees
18 Explorer of kids' TV
19 Steiger's role in "Jesus of Nazareth"
20 Twin-___ aircraft
22 Detected
23 Longtime RCA subsidiary
26 Pull out
27 Grandparents, often
30 Finger
31 Won big
34 Kurosawa's "___ in Fear"
35 Big Apple subway, familiarly, with "the"
36 Obstinate
38 Ask for milk?
39 "Darby ___ and the Little People": 1959 film
41 Hurricanes, e.g.
43 "Genuine Flabby Preludes (For a Dog)" composer
44 It has about 350,000 species
45 Noted Unitarian William ___ Channing
47 Literary initials
48 Instrument for Julian Bream
52 Send flying
54 Spiritual guide
56 Improve in small increments
57 Do something
60 Some tributes
61 Academia metaphor
62 Pain, so to speak
63 Charming café site, often

DOWN
1 Gets ready
2 Velma's rival in "Chicago"
3 Yucca fiber
4 Where you might be off your rocker
5 ___ on the head
6 Bearing gifts?
7 Big stretch
8 Unsettle
9 Upper hand
10 Challenging years
11 Extreme
12 In the past
13 Studied
14 Commercial updates

21 "The Lawrence Welk Show" sponsor

24 Smear

25 English muffin look-alike

28 Vigilant

29 Flat substitutes that are round

31 Call it quits

32 Subject of Justinian's reform

33 Expressway features

37 Reporters' needs

40 Criminal's undoer, informally

42 Early satellite built at Bell Labs

46 Mythical giants

49 Helpful

50 "A Confederacy of Dunces" author

51 "Ninotchka" director Lubitsch

53 Norah's father

55 Zwei multiple

58 Razz

59 Brogan letters

83

BY MYLES CALLUM

ACROSS

1 Traffic stopper, for some
10 Fresh, in a way
15 Rec room piece
16 Drift
17 Old-fashioned family reference
18 Fifth wheel
19 "Custom blended" gas seller
20 Chivalrous title
22 U.K. awards
23 Nobody special
25 Mall attraction
26 Pit-___
30 Pass opening
31 Use for nourishment
33 Tropical evergreen
35 Old bandleader with the catch phrase "That's right—you're wrong!"
37 Decommissioned flier
38 Like most early Beatles hits
40 At bay
42 Auto racer Fabi
43 Army leader for nearly 50 years
45 Birch of "American Beauty"
46 Verdi title bandit

48 Fresh
50 Tot's "little"
51 Made in the U.S.
52 In the first place?
55 It smells
56 Hollywood VIP
57 Like Beethoven's Ninth
62 Relatives of crane flies
64 Staff miniature
66 Disney World has a Loch Ness monster made of them
67 The Cyclones of the Big 12
68 "___ Hollywood": '80s magazine show
69 U.S. capital before New York City

DOWN

1 APB nos.
2 Waimea Bay's island
3 Some feds
4 "The Mysterious Island" captain
5 Rival of ancient Carthage
6 Stonewallers?
7 Air rifle ammo
8 Puzzling
9 Pine product
10 Short change?
11 Peace
12 Poorly situated
13 Gloaters' counterparts
14 Contemporary

170

21 Direct
24 Its coat of arms has a husky on it
26 It's less than right
27 Bills
28 Behave appropriately
29 Menlo Park monogram
32 Latin I word
34 Arab League member
36 "Card Players Quarreling" artist
39 Asked a lot of questions
41 Letter following upsilon
44 Mistaken
47 Playground retort
49 Certain neopagan
53 "Take note, man"
54 Valuable place?
58 Not fooled by
59 Stable shade
60 Ltr. directive
61 Actor Cobb
63 Box "a" on the IRS W-2
65 Impress, plus

84

BY BONNIE L. GENTRY

ACROSS

1 Isn't square
5 "I Got Life" musical
9 Not limited
14 Brother of Brynhild, in Icelandic myth
15 Beseeched
17 Cross
18 Useful online tally
19 Weddell Sea phenomenon
20 "Seven Year Ache" singer Cash
21 "Prose ___": Icelandic poetic manual
22 High-class achievements?
25 Cobb and others
26 Census data
27 Decided not to sell
31 Clever stroke
33 ___ Novo: Benin capital
34 Swedish entrepreneur Kreuger
35 Supreme Court justice Black, 1937–71
36 Pretoria's land: Abbr.
37 Creature on a Hawaiian crossing sign
38 Morales of "Southern Cross"
39 Simple life?

41 Eat (at)
42 Lt. Worf portrayer
43 Put in hot water, maybe
44 Loop initials
45 Break, in Bristol
47 Accordingly
48 Support vociferously
51 Clanton foe of 1881
52 Reception desk convenience
56 Eleanor Roosevelt's real first name
57 Grade components
58 Kept in the loop, briefly
59 Guinness Book listings
60 "___: My Story": C&W autobiography
61 Offering word

DOWN

1 Almost irrelevant
2 "See?" follower
3 Checkup item
4 Popular cut?
5 Cauldron tender
6 V-mail handler
7 NYSE debut
8 Too bad
9 Hallowed
10 Progress obstacle
11 God attended by Valkyries
12 Routing letters
13 Helping
16 "The Tempest" king

22 Snake of southwestern Europe

23 Eye

24 New parents' travel need

28 Toss-up

29 Oscar-nominated "Peyton Place" actress, 1957

30 Filled one's flush, perhaps

32 Indicated

39 Court

40 Drillers' gp.

46 Chain named for its founders, the Raffel brothers

47 Show

48 Pan handler

49 Socks

50 Film feline

53 Macavity's creator, initially

54 Wagerers' mecca: Abbr.

55 Cryptanalysis gp.

85

BY BARRY C. SILK

ACROSS

1 Base
7 Island north of Dar es Salaam
15 Like some rolls
16 Fads and such
17 Storage item
18 Undergo training, perhaps
19 Jack of westerns
20 Some boas
22 Hematological system
23 Adjust a document setting
25 Albemarle Sound site: Abbr.
26 Hot spot
27 ___ Miguel, largest of the Azores
28 "It's ___ sort of memory that only works backward": Carroll
30 Scut owners
31 JFK served in it
32 Letter string
33 Shock
34 4/25/1978 Veterans Stadium debut
40 Da or ja
41 First: Abbr.
42 Country surrounding Lesotho: Abbr.
43 Accord rival

46 Gay leader?
47 Folks
48 "___ ye not yon hills and dales": "The Gypsy Laddie"
49 "Unionism and Socialism" author
50 "And you, Miss, are no lady!" speaker
52 Puzzle
53 Sullen
55 Ottoman honorific
56 Holland Perry in "The Other," e.g.
58 One acting on impulse?
60 Below the surface
61 Remove deposits from, as a water heater
62 Hambletonian entrants
63 Sonnet part

DOWN

1 Dries out
2 Tethered
3 Tubes on the table
4 Bane of liberal religion
5 Ristorante ending
6 Salon supplies
7 Discounted investments
8 Like some simple cells
9 Senator, e.g., for short
10 Two pieces of pizza?
11 Babysitter's handful
12 Beverly Hills neighbor
13 Fit to be tilled

14 Versatile fibers
21 Fed. security
24 Soup grain
26 Supergirl's name on Krypton
29 Trident-shaped letters
30 Jet home
33 Word on two Monopoly squares
35 Kithara relative
36 Part of a Forbes "Richest Americans" name
37 Charles Portis novel made into a 1969 Western

38 Has gone out
39 Low-tech clicker
43 Concealed
44 Invariably
45 Arizona neighbor
46 Like "Psycho," and then some
49 Divine, in a way
51 Booties
53 ___ Helens: Abbr.
54 Intentions
57 Judge's decision
59 Wide width

86

BY ROBERT H. WOLFE

ACROSS

1 "Hmmm ..."
16 1924 novel whose 1995 book club edition had elephants on the cover
17 Traveler's memento
18 Looker
19 Academic aides, briefly
20 Company with an Effektiv storage furniture line
21 Critical
23 Mass. hours
25 Newly
28 Subtle smear
33 "And a Voice to Sing With" autobiographer
34 Known only to a select few
36 Wall St. specialist
37 When one might leave JFK
38 "Ninotchka" actress Claire
39 Fancier and then some
40 Deserved
41 "___ see it ..."
42 Astronomical staple
44 Impractical
45 Hot Wheels product
47 Lamb servings
49 Victorian leader?
50 Long range
52 Bitterness
55 Writer Rosten
56 "Should ___ ..."
59 Snaps unpredictably, say
64 Send back
65 Hard-to-reach places

DOWN

1 Drain
2 Old TV redhead
3 Nantucket-born retailer
4 "The Breakfast Club" actor
5 Headaches, oy vey
6 When repeated after "Hardy," Hanna-Barbera hyena
7 "Can ___ witness?"
8 Lalitpur denizens
9 '60s Ferrari classics
10 One might be received on a bridge
11 Go in smoothly
12 Stir up
13 State bordered by the Big Sioux River: Abbr.
14 Take on
15 "Blah ..."
22 Good thing not to be on
23 Braved
24 Haggis ingredient
25 Crosswind direction, at sea
26 1980 DeLuise film
27 Updated

29 Low square
30 Conductor Boulanger
31 "Advise and Consent" author
32 Conforms
35 California wine valley
38 Baseless
43 Roman magistrate
44 Takes for granted
46 Balance
48 Soul-searching effort?
51 Dame modifier?

52 Celtic hero
53 "Understood"
54 Period of effectiveness
55 English soprano Felicity
57 Role for Teri
58 Attacked, as a project, with "into"
60 Enzyme ending
61 Thing in court
62 Continental trade org.
63 Paris's Pont ___ Arts

87

BY DOUG PETERSON

ACROSS

1 Threw a ball
7 Climax
15 His 262 hits in 2004 set a single-season Major League record
16 High
17 Many an ex-lib
18 Petitioner
19 Some ales
20 Values that divide a statistical sample into four equal parts
21 Like the WTO
22 Bounder
23 Interstate through Houston
24 Result of an open-door policy?
27 Raised area
31 60 minuti
32 Moon of Uranus
34 Short
35 Donut shop freebie
38 One working on the RR
39 Causing a buzz
40 One causing a buzz
41 Calliope power
43 Disappoints
45 Start of an apology
47 One of a peppery trio?
48 "I haven't got any troubles I can't tell standing up" speaker
50 Bought generously
54 Clinton Labor secretary Robert
55 Bootee fillers
56 Storage spot
57 It established a bicameral legislature
58 Hold high
59 Box for bags
60 In the saddle

DOWN

1 Language that gives us "shampoo"
2 On the beach
3 Limited in scope
4 Get to giggle
5 Lover of Psyche
6 Family figure
7 Residency requirement, often
8 A ukulele might accompany it
9 Bridget Riley's "Blaze 4," e.g.
10 Toothpaste catchword
11 Island north of Martinique
12 Unwritten
13 Table ___
14 Expos, since 2005
20 Fall out
22 Loft user

25 Belgian Grand Prix town
26 Eponymous seismologist Charles
28 Old built-in kitchen convenience
29 Its opening includes a brief "American Gothic" parody
30 Nice being
31 People
33 Developed

36 Thespian
37 JFK posting
42 Admirable person
44 Entertaining the idea of
46 Quick on the uptake
49 Rum, for some
50 Holds or saves
51 Leaf opening
52 Personnel list
53 Tolls
54 Devil-may-care
56 Type of patch

88

BY KAREN M. TRACEY

ACROSS

1 Be visually subtle
11 Dirty Harry's org.
15 It's shaken but not stirred
16 Lessen
17 True love
18 Way to go
19 Hague Convention subject
20 Policy end
21 Spade and others
22 Imitate
23 First name in toasting?
26 P.D. rank
27 Kind of beauty?
28 Vocalist Anderson who sang with Ellington
30 "Women in Love" author
32 Seat of Dallas County, Alabama
34 Dog's age
35 Taken in
36 Hearing need
39 Workout target
40 Fixes a backsplash, perhaps
41 Director Jean-___ Godard
43 "Kidnapped" monogram
44 Cast out
45 Popular branch of yoga
47 Like pangolins
48 Retreats
52 ___ Valley: site where "Poltergeist" was filmed
53 Main network
54 Flight deck forecasts, briefly
55 Gossip
56 Bad impression?
57 At all

DOWN

1 Put (away)
2 Zola heroine
3 Like some profs.
4 One way to be taken
5 Germany's Adenauer
6 Went over carefully
7 Titan who stole fire from the gods
8 One, to 5-Down
9 Lab svc.
10 It'll get you in
11 Pioneer
12 Multifunction office purchase
13 Joint quarters
14 Tide and Surf
20 Manchester measure
22 Paw's partner
23 Made to appear faded, as fabric
24 Stimulate and then some

180

25 Subject of a Lexington statue, generally speaking

27 Beneficiary of a 1971 Harrison/Shankar concert

29 Online communications forum

31 City near Ben Gurion airport

33 Back way

37 President Bartlet, familiarly, on "The West Wing"

38 Muse with a flute

42 Union site

45 Combo's cue

46 "Bird on ___": Gibson movie

48 1944 Chemistry Nobelist

49 Capital on Upolu Island

50 Itches

51 U.S. Army E-6

53 It marked the beginning of the "Lost Generation"

1

```
A T   T I M E S   A D V E R B S
L O W T E C H   L E I S U R E
B R I S T L E   L A C O N I C
I R S   S A R D I N E   A G E
N E T S   T I R E S   A M A D
O N E T O   D A D   A B O D E
S T R A W H A T   A W A K E S
      M I E N   B I A S
Q U A I N T   B E D C H E C K
U S I N G   P E W   S E G A L
A T R A   C R E A K   D O N E
S I B   B R I N I E R   I N E
A N A G R A M   L E A D S O N
R O S E A T E   E N T I T L E
S V E L T E R   D E E P S I X
```

2

```
S H A N N O N   G A S M A S K
P E T N A M E   A T T A C H E
C R A W D A D   B L A R N E Y
A E R   I N S U L A R   E D S
  S I G N   N E S T
    L E O V I   T U N I C S
E T T A   T O T O   P I N O N
R A H S   C L A R E   E T R E
G R A S P   T R E E   C O K E
S A T Y R S   I L L B E
    E L B A   U S S R
S P A   G U R N E Y S   H E E
K I L D A R E   L E T T E R S
A T T E M P T   H A L I B U T
T H E B E S T   I R E L A N D
```

3

```
C O D E W O R D S   S L O S H
O N O R A B O U T   L E T H E
R E M I N I S C E   O T T E R
N O I S E   S H E D   S O L O
C N N     E L E C T I V E
H O E   C L O S E S H A V E S
I N E   H E W S   P O L
P E R M I A N   C O R K I N G
    A N T   R A I D   M O O
C H U R C H B E L L S   P C T
H I T C H E R S   O H O
E T U I   R O O M   V I S A S
A T R A S   G R A P E V I N E
P E N N E   U T T E R A N C E
O R S O N   E S T R A N G E D
```

4

```
E A R F L A P   M I S N A M E
C H A R A D E   E M P O R I A
R E M I N D S   W A L T E R S
U M P   G U E S S T I M A T E
    D E P T H   T E S H
A F A R   A I M T O
T A K I N G   P E E P H O L E
O L I V I E R   D R E A M O N
Z A N E G R E Y   I N R O A D
    H E M A N   E O N S
  P S S T   R E A L M
R A T T L E S N A K E   S S E
O N A R O L L   R I D E O U T
M E L A N I E   B R I E F E R
P L E D G E D   Y A N G T Z E
```

5

```
S C A R A B   C A R D G A M E
C H U B B Y   A C A D E M I C
R A D I U M   I M P E R I A L
A L I S   A G N E S   M A H I
P I T   A I L     B A P
E C O   B L A N C S   A L M S
S E R I F   R E L E A S E M E
      R A R E E A R T H
L O V E B E A D S   R E A D S
O D E S   S T A P L E   N O H
C D S     E O E   I M A
U S P S   D O N D I   E M I R
S H E S M I N E   T I R A N E
T O R T O N I S   E D I T O R
S E S S I O N S   R E C E S S
```

6

```
L I C K   S H A L E   S O A K
I D E A   A E S O P   E L L E
B O L T   T R I N I   E D G Y
E L L   T O B A C C O S H O P
R A U C O U S   H U G   A R A
A T L A S T   G A R R O T E D
C R A M S   M I N U E T
E Y R E   B O L E S   O T I S
    B R A N D Y   P O I N T
G R A Y A R E A   H E L E N A
E E N   I C Y   T I R E O U T
I N K B L O T T E S T   N E E
S O A R   D R O P S   T E N T
H I R E   E E R I E   S O D A
A R A L   S E N D S   K N O X
```

7

```
S W A S H B U C K L E   O F T
C A P T A I N H O O K   R I O
A R L E S F R A N C E   I V Y
R E E L   F I R   A D A G E
P S A L M   G L U T   L I C E
    A E S   O N E L I N E R
E T A   T H A T I   A V A N T
M A R I E A N T O I N E T T E
M I C R O   G E N O A   E S S
A L L E R G I C   N I P
S P I N   L O O M   S A M B A
  I G E T A   R I P   L A R S
H E H   B R I D L E L A N E S
A C T   S E M A N T I C I A N
Y E S   P R A Y E R B E A D S
```

8

```
B A D N E W S   C S L E W I S
A T H E A R T   L E O N I N E
S H A D R O E   A L S O R A N
H O R   S T P A U L S   E S T
E M M A   E O N S     H E R
D E A N S   N E E D A   A N I
      A W A I T   U P R I S E
T O P M A S T   S P H E R E S
U N R E S T   S T E I N
G P O   H I P P O   D A V I T
O A F   L E V I   L E M A
F R O   M A I D E N S   R P M
W O R D A G E   T A K E N U P
A L M O N E R   O N A D A T E
R E A R E R S   P E T A L E D
```

9

```
.EGG.SAC..SALSA
ICER.TRON.ATEAM
MOTA.ALFA.LLANO
PLANETOFTHEAPES
SETUP..ELMAN...
...LIEGE.OBTAIN
.MOA.RATA.LIBRE
VICTORIASSECRET
OTHER.ABES..MAD
ATODDS.LARGO...
...SEINE..ANKLE
ARTURRUBINSTEIN
GAUGE.LONE.HYMN
EMBAR.LODE.LENS
SPARS.KYD.YDS..
```

10

```
ECONOMICWARFARE
VEGETABLEMARROW
ASLOOSEASAGOOSE
STENO.TNT.INNER
...SLO..END....
QTS.ENS.ORG.BAA
AHAB.SPINALCORD
TELEPHONESYSTEM
AMELIORATE.ACTE
REM.CRT.ORB.HEN
....TAE..SAD...
EMBER.TWI.SAHIB
DOAROARINGTRADE
GAINONESFREEDOM
ENTENTECORDIALE
```

11

```
LINEDUP.LOWDOWN
ANEMONE.AMRADIO
STPETER.MAIDENS
SEARS.ICANT..SKI
ORLY.OSH..EASEL
ERE.ABHORS.LADY
DOSAGE.PETAL...
.REDEYESPECIAL.
...ADEPT.VENDOR
PROP.DAISES.LIE
RENTA..CNN.LISP
IDS.SHAKO.PABLO
DRIFTER.OPENBAR
EATDIRT.TENCENT
SWEARBY.SPHERES
```

12

```
IMPS.ORDINARIES
LIRE.SHORELEAVE
EXIT.COCKAMAMIE
NEVADANS..SCALP
ERASURE.DEBT...
..TINS.YUGOSLAV
SUEDE.LORAX.AXE
TREE.OAKEN.CULT
YAY.DOZER.MODES
ELEGIZED.MOLE..
...ACED.WOODROW
ALERT.THURSDAY.
FORDUMMIES.NASA
ROLEMODELS.ALIT
OPENSESAME.PEST
```

13

```
MOLOTOV.AMASSES
INARAGE.PATIENT
DABBLES.PRORATA
DDE.LETSLIP.LEG
LALA.SEPIA.BANG
ERECT.DEE.DANTE
CERTIFIEDLETTER
..RAINDROPS....
SILENTTREATMENT
IREST.EES.HAVER
DONS.BRAES.NASA
ENS.DUEDATE.STD
BACKERS.REPTILE
AGAINST.CLEAVER
REPASTS.HEELERS
```

14

```
ATBEST.REF.SOPH
PHRASE.ALE.ELEA
REASSEMBLE.MERL
IONE..ABE.MISDO
ORA.STINGO.TIE.
REGGAE..ALFRED
IMHENRYVIIIIAM
..NOREASTER....
.HERMANSHERMITS
COMEAT..RESTON
ALI.LEARNS.SUE
LEROY.LEA..MOTE
LOAD.VOLGARIVER
AUTO.AHA.CAMERA
STER.TAX.THIRST
```

15

```
STARSHAPED.APTS
COMICOPERA.DRAW
ATIGHTSPOT.JOKE
BEDSORE.SEDUCEE
...LOSS.BAREST
SPREAD.PLAYEDAT
CRIER.ALECS.USA
ROSE.PLINK.OREL
AMI.BRAND.BREAK
PENPOINT.JOISTS
ENGRAM.SCUM...
SATIRIC.RIBBONE
ODIE.NAMECALLER
FEDS.GRAPESUGAR
FRET.SPEEDTRAPS
```

16

```
STRIKEZONE.ALIS
PRIVATELAW.SANE
EATENALIVE.ESSE
ACT.LIVERPATES
REEFS.GESSO.NAT
SYRIAN...LHASA
.TREETOP.AMOR
BALTIMORERAVENS
ULEE.ONEROSE...
SPADE...VINYLS
RAN.PAOLO.ASEAT
ICEFISHING.SUR
DIDO.TALIASHIRE
ENOS.ORANGEADES
SONS.RECESSIONS
```

17

```
TACO.CATTLECALL
OLAV.AVERAGEJOE
RARE.CATAMARANS
AMER.ASE..DEMIT
HOTSPOT.MISS...
..APR.ROD...GTS
LIKEAHOUSEAFIRE
ABENDINTHERIVER
WORDONTHESTREET
SSS..GAS..SSN..
...WEEP.DAYTONA
MAKES..JAL.STIR
ONEATATIME.TICS
MARVELOVER.ECHO
STRESSTEST.PEEN
```

18

```
TURNSLOOSE.CMON
ANOUKAIMEE.HONE
MISTITLING.ONTV
POS.RESTS.ALOHA
ANIMUS.ENTERED.
..ANTES.ERRATA
.PARS.DEBRA.IAN
BOLT.AIRED.ELKS
LOA.UNTIL.SASE
ALBINO.FLATT..
STAMINA.MASSED
TAMPS.MASON.PLO
OBIE.MASKEDBALL
FLAN.ANTIBIOTIC
FEND.WAITANDSEE
```

19

```
MTN.CAFE.SAWOFF
THANATOS.AZALEA
GENERALS.NUGGET
.NOSEBLEEDSEATS
GASSY.ONAPAR...
ATE.OWER..SPA
BUCKEYE.SMUSHES
BROOKED.POPTOPS
LANDERS.LECARRE
ELD.UNIT..TAS
.LARIAT.GIRLS
CONSTITUTIONAL
IDCARD.SINFONIA
TOATEE.ENLARGER
ERASES.AGAR.EST
```

20

```
LARGEOJ.VOYAGES
ACOUPLE.IRONOUT
BROMIDE.RAWDATA
ROM.SIP.GTS.TER
ABIE.EERIE.LIRR
TAELS.REN.RASPE
STRINGSATTACHED
.IPCRESS....
AUDITORSREPORTS
TROTS.EUR.SHEET
OBOE.SEPIA.OVER
MAD.LAP.TLC.ONA
INAHOLE.OBERLIN
SIDECAR.RELIVED
TVSPOTS.YELPERS
```

21

```
LIMPBIZKIT.OPUS
INELEGANCE.LIKE
MONOTONIES.ILEX
ANDY..ENSLAVE
..STAGE.AMIDST
SOL.HUR..BEREA
NNE.ERES.ERRING
ORA.JAYLENO.VAG
RADIUS.ONUS.ETE
EMEND..TRI.RED
SPRAGS.DREAM
.SWEEPEA..AHAS
ASHE.NONCHALANT
OHIO.DOTTEDLINE
KOPF.SPEEDDEMON
```

22

```
FOREFATHER.SCAB
ICEMACHINE.NARY
STAIRCASES.ASTA
TARTLETS.CHIPIN
...ESS.QUALIFY
SPLAYS.FUEL.AIM
TOON.ETUI.FENCE
ALOT.SHREW.ASIA
TAKEN.ROTO.SEAN
ERA.ODER.ROYALS
FIGTREE.PER
ATHOME.LETSLIDE
CIAO.PEASHOOTER
TEST.EDITINGOUT
SSTS.NONONSENSE
```

23

```
OPENANDSHUTCASE
ROYALCOPENHAGEN
ELECTORALDEFEAT
OSHA.END..EELS
.ORS..MOS...
BSH.SUBJOIN.AVA
UHOH.ALANSEEGER
LOWERSONESGUARD
BADHAIRDAY.RIDE
SLY.JOEBLOW.NIN
.SAN.UAE....
ALEC.ESL.GASH
CARRIERAIRGROUP
ITTAKESAVILLAGE
DEEPESTRECESSES
```

24

```
BASEMAN.GARNISH
ATHLETE.OCEANIA
SHALLOW.TEMPLES
SOMETIMES..ANT
OLE.ONONESWAY
.SNOWDRIFT...
POPCORN.ENFORCE
ARGOTS.JOVIAL
TRAFFIC.PARENTS
.FINALISTS...
BURSTOPEN.DDE
ONO.SACAJAWEA
AIMEDAT.ENAMELS
STAMINA.REVOLVE
TENSION.STARTED
```

25

L	A	L	A	L	A		J	A	Z	Z	E	D	U	P
A	V	A	L	O	N		S	W	E	E	T	I	S	H
B	E	Y	O	N	D		T	A	L	K	O	V	E	R
O	M	A	N	I		P	R	I	D	E		I	D	A
H	A	N	G		Q	U	O	T	A		G	N	U	S
E	R	E		F	U	N	K	S		C	R	E	P	E
M	I	G	R	A	I	N	E		S	H	E			
E	A	G	E	R	L	Y		J	A	I	A	L	A	I
			M	E	T		F	U	L	L	T	I	L	T
R	A	B	I	D		C	O	N	T	I		G	I	S
E	M	I	T		M	U	R	K	Y		C	H	E	N
W	I	N		B	E	R	R	Y		E	A	T	N	O
I	N	A	S	E	N	S	E		J	U	N	E	A	U
N	O	R	E	A	S	O	N		C	R	E	S	T	S
D	R	Y	Q	U	A	R	T		T	O	A	T	E	E

26

R	E	M	A	N	D			S	C	O	F	F	S	
E	L	E	M	E	N	T		D	R	O	P	O	U	T
H	O	L	Y	W	A	R		A	A	M	I	L	N	E
A	P	O		S	T	E	R	N		A	N	D	E	R
B	E	T	S		E	L	A	T	E		E	E	R	O
	S	T	A		S	L	I	E	S	T		D	A	I
			Y	E	T	I	S		S	H	O	U	L	D
	C	I	N	C		S	E	N		A	M	P	S	
N	A	N	O	O	K		C	O	N	T	I			
E	M	T		L	O	C	A	T	E		T	W	A	
B	E	E	S		C	L	I	N	T		S	I	C	S
B	I	R	T	H		O	N	I	C	E		S	U	E
I	N	R	O	A	D	S		C	O	N	D	E	M	N
S	T	O	O	L	I	E		E	S	T	A	T	E	S
H	O	R	D	E	S				T	R	Y	O	N	E

27

B	E	S	T	S	E	L	L	E	R		C	H	E	F
O	N	T	H	E	L	O	O	S	E		R	A	N	A
S	T	A	I	R	C	A	S	E	S		A	N	T	I
H	O	R	N	R	I	M	S		T	E	N	D	E	R
			D	A	D	E		R	E	V	E	L	R	Y
C	A	B	O	T		D	U	O		A	D	E	P	T
A	L	L	W	E	T		P	L	A	N		B	R	A
S	P	A	N		W	I	P	E	S		R	A	I	L
T	I	C		P	O	R	E		A	V	E	R	S	E
I	N	K	L	E		O	D	D		A	P	S	E	S
G	E	L	A	T	I	N		A	A	R	E			
A	R	I	S	E	S		B	I	S	M	A	R	C	K
T	A	G	S		T	R	A	N	S	I	T	I	O	N
E	C	H	O		L	I	S	T	E	N	E	D	T	O
S	E	T	S		E	A	S	Y	S	T	R	E	E	T

28

W	I	S	E	C	R	A	C	K		B	E	A	S	T
I	N	T	R	O	U	B	L	E		O	N	T	H	E
S	T	R	I	K	E	O	I	L		D	E	L	O	N
D	R	A	K	E			P	S	I	S		A	R	P
O	O	N		S	L	O	P	E	D		D	R	E	I
M	I	G	S		O	X	E	Y	E		A	G	U	N
S	T	E	W	O	V	E	R		C	H	E	E	P	S
			A	V	E	S		S	L	E	D			
F	A	C	I	A	L		S	E	A	W	A	L	L	S
A	S	A	N		O	T	T	E	R		L	I	E	U
C	A	R	S		C	H	O	K	E	R		C	N	N
E	R	L		S	K	I	M		A	M	E	S	S	
O	U	T	D	O		R	A	I	N	D	A	N	C	E
F	L	O	O	R		S	C	R	E	A	M	S	A	T
F	E	N	C	E		T	H	E	C	R	E	E	P	S

29

L	I	S	A	M	A	R	I	E		S	L	O	S	H
A	T	P	R	E	S	E	N	T		M	A	F	I	A
S	H	I	F	T	L	E	S	S		E	R	I	C	S
H	E	N		H	A	L	O		B	L	A	N	K	S
			T	A	N	S		H	E	T		T	A	O
A	S	S	E	N	T		D	E	L	E	T	E	S	
S	W	O	R	E		S	E	M	I	R	U	R	A	L
P	E	C	S		A	L	F	I	E		B	E	D	E
S	E	C	E	S	S	I	O	N		B	I	S	O	N
	T	E	R	M	I	T	E		D	O	N	T	G	O
F	I	R		I	D	S		W	I	N	G			
R	E	B	A	T	E		B	A	S	K		M	S	S
O	P	A	R	T		W	A	S	H	E	D	O	U	T
M	I	L	N	E		A	R	T	E	R	I	O	L	E
M	E	L	O	N		D	R	E	S	S	E	D	U	P

30

M	O	S	S	B	A	C	K		S	U	F	F	I	X
O	N	T	H	E	R	U	N		U	N	I	O	N	S
B	L	U	E	N	O	S	E		S	I	E	R	R	A
S	E	M			O	P	A	R	T		F	R	A	N
T	A	P	E	S		D	I	A	S		E	N	D	
E	V	E	N	T		L	E	G	I	T		A	G	O
R	E	D	L	I	N	E	D		N	A	P	L	E	S
			A	P	E	X		B	E	T	A			
R	E	V	I	E	W		C	A	D	U	C	E	U	S
A	L	A		N	Y	L	O	N		T	E	M	P	T
N	E	C		D	O	E	R			E	R	O	D	E
S	C	A	M		R	E	B	U	T		T	A	W	
A	T	T	A	C	K		E	X	H	I	B	I	T	A
C	R	E	C	H	E		T	O	O	K	O	V	E	R
K	O	S	H	E	R		T	R	U	E	W	E	S	T

31

T	A	K	E	A	V	O	T	E		A	L	T	A	R
A	B	A	N	D	O	N	E	D		B	O	R	N	E
D	I	N	G	A	L	I	N	G		A	M	A	T	I
A	G	E	R		T	O	M	E		S	A	D	A	T
			R	A	N	I		R	E	N	E	G	E	
F	O	R	T	E		S	L	O	E	S		N	O	R
I	R	I	S	E	S		E	R	S		A	N	A	
R	I	P	P	L	E	S		R	E	A	D	M	I	T
	E	E	R		A	L	T		T	W	E	E	Z	E
E	N	O		C	R	Y	U	P		A	P	S	E	S
S	T	A	M	O	S		R	E	A	R				
C	A	R	A	S		I	M	E	T		H	O	S	E
A	T	I	L	T		N	O	V	E	L	E	T	T	E
P	E	N	T	A		D	I	E	S	E	L	O	I	L
E	D	G	A	R		O	L	D	T	I	M	E	R	S

32

S	E	V	E	N	S	E	A	S		O	R	C	A	S
P	R	I	M	I	T	I	V	E		R	E	E	S	E
R	A	N	S	C	A	R	E	D		A	G	A	P	E
A	T	E		E	V	E	R	E	S	T		S	I	S
T	O	D	A	T	E		T	R	O	O	P	E	R	S
			R	I	D	E			A	R	A	F	A	T
P	R	I	M	E		A	J	A	R		P	I	T	A
R	O	L	L	S		R	E	X		S	O	R	E	R
E	L	L	E		A	N	T	E		C	O	E	D	S
P	E	N	T	A	D			D	U	O	S			
A	M	A	S	S	I	N	G		S	U	E	D	E	D
R	O	T		S	T	A	R	L	E	T		U	R	I
E	D	U	C	E		R	A	I	S	E	C	A	I	N
R	E	R	U	N		E	N	D	U	R	A	N	C	E
S	L	E	E	T		S	T	O	P	S	D	E	A	D

33

```
J O E I S U Z U   R E B U T S
E N D N O T E S   A G A T H A
R A G T R A D E   T O P T E N
I D I O T   L E T S   E B B
C I E   A S W E L L   O R A L
H E S S   P O S S E   R E B A
O T T O M A N S   S L I D E S
      L I C K   S N E E
H A B I L E   C H A I N S A W
A B A D   C R O O K   T H R O
D A B S   A D O R E D   A S U
A L Y   S D A K   A S P E N
N O S A L E   O P E N M I N D
I N A R U T   F O R T E R I E
P E T E R S   F I R E W O O D
```

34

```
S C A T T E D   I N S T E A D
P O L E A X E   N I T R A T E
H U M E R A L   S H E A R E R
E T A   A C T I I   W I L L A
R U N S   T A N S   L O I N
E R A T O   S A T A T   B E G
D E C A D E   C O M E H E R E
      L E S S O N O N E
G O G E T T E R   S T A R E R
O R R   S E E N A   S T O L E
O V I D   D E M O   H U M P
F I N E D   B R I D E   L T R
O L D T I M E   D E C L A R E
F L E E C E D   S T R I D E S
F E R R E T S   T O U P E E S
```

35

```
N O T A B L Y   C A S I N O S
I R O N I E S   I T E R A N T
A I R E D A L E T E R R I E R
G O R G E D   A R A B   V I A
A L E G   B R U T   T E R I
R E N   S L A T S   S I T O N
A S T O N I S H   K A R E N S
      C E A S E F I R E
M I S T E R   N O W A D A Y S
A N W A R   S W A I N   M A T
K A E L   S H A M   T A R E
E R A   A M O R   A G E N D A
W A T E R O V E R T H E D A M
A G I T A T E   C O I N A G E
R E T A P E D   A M A S S E D
```

36

```
P I A F   A B O D Y   V I E S
I T S O   M U N R O   E N Y A
C H A R L O T T E R U S S E S
T E N S E S T   S K A T E R S
      A A A   O P S   R I V
R O L L   E N E R O   G E M S
I N T E R D E P E N D E N C E
N I E   A I D   H E E   T R A
S O R R Y T O H E A R T H A T
E N N E   S N E A D   R H E O
      A F T   E R R   T I E
E S T E E M S   S E E P A G E
W E I R D A L Y A N K O V I C
E A V E   Y I E L D   L E F T
S M E E   I P A S S   I N T O
```

37

```
C H O P S H O P   S Y S O P S
S O N A T I N A   P U L L E T
H O T W A T E R   E R O I C A
A V I S   I N T H A T   V A N
R E M   S T O N E R S   E N D
P R E S T O   E I S   P O P I
      W A F E R S   P A Y I N
B R E A K F A S T T A B L E S
R A M I E   R I S E R S
A D I N   C T N   L E T S G O
D I G   G R A C K L E   P I C
P A R   R E G R E T   D I M E
I T A L I A   I S A B E L L A
T O T A L S   M E L A L L E N
T R E B L E   E Y E T E S T S
```

38

```
P R E F A C E S   I S E U L T
R A V I G O T E   N A R R O W
O V E R G R O W   A F R I C A
P E N S I O N S   B A S S O S
      T E N   S I R
T E A S   A S T O N I S H E D
W I L T   S T R A D   P U M A
E D G E   O A K   A N E W
R E A P   E D D I E   C A N E
P R E S S A G E N T   E N D S
      C R Y   A B C
W I S D O M   S A G U A R O S
E D W I N A   O V E R D O N E
S E A R E R   W O R K E D U P
T S K T S K   S W E E T E S T
```

39

```
V F W H A L L S   B A G J O B
C R I E S O U T   A I R A C E
R E L A T I V E   C R O W E D
T E L L E R   P O K E   B A P
A M I   R E C O U P   M O N O
P E E R   A N T E   A N I S
E N S E M B L E   D I R E C T
      F O O L   M A L T
S H B O O M   T A L L Y M A N
M O O R   B O H R   R O T E
A T O M   S L A L O M   U P S
L L D   P H A T   S I G N E T
L I L L I E   S U M T O T A L
O N E I L L   I N A T R I C E
J E S S E L   T E N S P E E D
```

40

```
S T A R T U P   I S R A E L I
P A T E R N O   S T A N D I N
E N T A I L S   T I N C A N S
A N I   B I T P A R T   S S T
K E M P   T E E N S   S N E E
T R E E D   D A B   S T E E P
O Y S T E R   C U S T A R D
      I N T H E L E A D
B O O T E E S   P R I E S T
M A U L S   X I S   R U L E R
A R T E   L A G O S   M I C E
I C I   R E G N A N T   T R A
L O N G A G O   R O A D I E S
E D G E S I N   E R N E S T O
R E S E A T S   R E G I M E N
```

41

```
C A T S M E O W . . F L A I R
I N A P I N C H . F I E R C E
T E X A S T E A . I N A S E C
A M I N O . A L B E E . E P I
D O C . S N E L L . S N I P .
E N A M E L . R E D . N I C E
L E B A N O N . A T T A C K S
. T Y P E . C R O P . . . . .
T S T R A P S . H I B A C H I
O T H O . Y S L . P Y T H O N
S E E N . J E E P S . A T F .
P E R . J O N A H . T A S S O
A P O G E E . N O M A T T E R
R E B U T S . O N S T R E A M
E D E N S . . N Y G I A N T S
```

42

```
N A G N A G . L A P . H E S .
O T O O L E . O N A S L A N T
O P E N I N G S E N T E N C E
S A S . S A L E M . R A G O N
E R O S . S O S O . A K I M .
. V I A . M O N E Y . N P R .
S E N N A . N E T . A G A R .
S T R E T C H E S A C R O S S
O R T S . M A S . L O I N S .
D O H . D E N T E . T S E . .
. N E R O . D E L S . E S T A
A G W A Y . S M I T S . H I P
S T A T E D E P A R T M E N T
S E L E N I T E . O L D A G E
T A L . . S S R . M O L D E R
```

43

```
P A T S Y . J A C K F R O S T
U S A I R . A T A G L A N C E
L I L T S . B A R B A R I A N
L A K E . O B L A . A N N E .
A M I . F L E E C E D . E S T
P I N . E E R . A D E E . . .
A N G O R A S . S U N D E C K
R O T O R . . . T A L O N . .
T R O P I C S . T H I M B L E
. S E R E . H O N . O D E . .
A D O . D O T T I N G . W A S
D E S I . . F A R E . O R S O
A B C S P O R T S . S T O I C
M I A M I H E A T . S T O C K
S T R E A M E R S . T O M E S
```

44

```
F A S T B U C K . C I P H E R
R U N O U T O N . O R I O L E
I R A N G A T E . M A T T E D
T E R I S . T A M E S . L A W
T A L . F A D E S . M I N I .
E T A L I I . S T A . A N O N
R E T O R T S . I C E B E R G
. . V E T O . E R L E . . . .
R O B E S O N . R O L L B A R
O N E I . B O W . S A L O M E
A L E N . E R I C S . R A P .
D E F . S T A S H . T H E T A
M A I T A I . D I O M E D E S
A V E N G E . O R D E R O U T
P E R N O D . M R A N D M R S
```

45

```
P I B B . C A C A O . A S I F
A G R A . O M A N I . S I D E
P O I S O N P E N L E T T E R
A R C A N A . N E W F O U N D
. K L E I N . S E R R A T E .
C A S T I R O N . L E S T . .
E M A I L . D I A L M . I R S
L I N C . P A S T S . N O A H
L E D . P O L A R . G O N Z O
. M E R S . N I G H T C A P .
V I O L E T S . A R E S O . .
E N R A G I N G . A N O M I E
N A T I O N A L A N T H E M S
O N A N . G R E E T . O D A S
M E R E . S E E R S . T Y N E
```

46

```
I M I N . B A T H T U B G I N
C O N E . A R M O R P L A T E
E T N A . P E A C E P I P E S
C O A T . T N N . A S T E R S
A R M E N I A . S T A . . . .
S C E N E S . S T Y L I S T S
T O O . E M B E R . A C C R A
L A N G . S A X O N . C O A L
E C L A T . R E M A P . R D A
S H Y L O C K S . K A R E E M
. . P A S . C E R E B R A . .
O R M O L U . C O D . G O O N
T O O N E S F A C E . G A U D
I N D I S A R R A Y . A R T E
C A S T S L O O S E . E D E R
```

47

```
S W E A T H O G . M O T I F S
E A R P H O N E . A L L N E W
C L A R I N E T . T I C K L E
E L S . N E W S M E N . S T A
D E E R S . A S I S . S P U R
E T R E . D Y E S . I H O P S
. . S C O T T S . N I T T I .
W H A T A M I . T R E A S O N
H O F F A . C O H O S T . . .
I N F U N . K N E W . S I N S
T O L L . H E E P . R U N U P
E L I . P E T I O L E . T A R
O U C H E S . D I A L T O N E
U L T R A S . A N N E R I C E
T U S S L E . S T A T U T E S
```

48

```
S M E L T S . F U L L S T O P
H O N E Y S . O N E O N O N E
O N T A P E . L I N G E R E R
W A I V E . F L O . S A R I S
S U R E . P R O N G . D I D O
O R E . G R O W S U P . D A N
F A T T I E S T . S E E . . .
F L Y O F F T H E H A N D L E
. A T E . E N E R G I E S . .
M O N . S C A L E R S . S A C
A R E A . T E E M S . G A G A
G I B E D . R A Y . G A S U P
M O U S E P A D . P O R T I A
A L L O C A T E . U N B E N D
S E A P O W E R . G E O R G E
```

49

```
A T A N A N G L E ▓ ▓ A T T S
C A N O P E N E R ▓ A M E R E
C R I M E W A V E ▓ D O N U T
R O S E ▓ T W I ▓ G E S T E S
A T E ▓ S E N S U A L ▓ A L A
▓ ▓ ▓ D O S ▓ ▓ ▓ T R E E T O P
S I L E N T ▓ R E D ▓ R I V A
P L E A ▓ A M U S E ▓ E V E R
A L A R ▓ M A G ▓ N I C E S T
C A T E R E R ▓ T N T ▓ ▓ ▓
E T H ▓ A N C H O R S ▓ A M O
S E E F I T ▓ E S O ▓ S L A B
O A R E D ▓ D R A W A L I N E
U S E A S ▓ T A K E S I D E S
T E R R ▓ ▓ S T A L E M A T E
```

50

```
T O W N S ▓ C A M P S ▓ I T U P
O D E O N ▓ A M E R I C A N A
M E A D E ▓ T U N A M E L T S
A T S E A ▓ C L A N S ▓ K A T
S T E A K ▓ H E C K ▓ V E N I
▓ A L L S T A T E ▓ W E D G E
▓ ▓ ▓ U R L S ▓ M O G U L S
S C A L P E L ▓ P A R A P E T
P A T I O S ▓ T A L L ▓ ▓ ▓
O R T O N ▓ S H R E D D E R
K O A N ▓ K T E L ▓ C E L E B
E L I ▓ E M O T E ▓ L A M A R
F I N D S A W A Y ▓ A R O M A
O N E S T R I K E ▓ S I R E S
R E D L E T T E R ▓ S E E D S
```

51

```
A S T O R I A ▓ R E S H A P E
N O R M A N S ▓ O T T O M A N
G R E A T S A L T D E S E R T
E V E R S ▓ N U T ▓ T E R R A
L I T S ▓ S A L E S ▓ D I I I
I N O ▓ A T L U N C H ▓ G E L
C O P Y C A T ▓ T H E B O S S
▓ ▓ M E R E ▓ O M I T ▓ ▓
S W E A R E R ▓ T E N U R E D
T E A ▓ B A N S H E E ▓ A M Y
E T T E ▓ T A K E R ▓ G R I N
A W I N K ▓ T I C ▓ G E E N A
M A N D A R I N O R A N G E S
U S T I N O V ▓ R E L I A N T
P H O N E M E ▓ E N L I S T S
```

52

```
A D O S ▓ S T E A M P O W E R
D E N T ▓ T I A C A R R E R E
A F A R ▓ I N T I M I D A T E
M O R A L E S ▓ D I V I N E D
S L A K E S ▓ C L E A N ▓ ▓
A I M E D ▓ H A Y ▓ T A P E S
P A P S ▓ R E V ▓ R E L I S T
P T A ▓ A E R A T E S ▓ N P R
L O G O F F ▓ L A X ▓ W A L E
E R E C T ▓ E R G ▓ C O C A S
▓ ▓ T E R R Y ▓ T A L O N S
E M P E R O R ▓ M U D F L A T
N E A T A S A P I N ▓ M A D E
T A T T L E T A L E ▓ A D E S
S T E E L Y A R D S ▓ N A S T
```

53

```
S P A C E B A R ▓ A R A B I C
H O T H O U S E ▓ R O M E R O
A T R A N D O M ▓ L E A D O N
W H I R ▓ D N A T E S T I N G
L O F T S ▓ E K E S ▓ Z O A
E L L ▓ A R M E D ▓ O D E U M
D E E P S E A S ▓ B R O N T E
▓ ▓ ▓ E S P N ▓ D O I N ▓ ▓
A R I S E S ▓ R E D E E M E D
D E C O R ▓ S E V E N ▓ E R E
D D E ▓ D A L I ▓ T O T A L
O F F T H E W A L L ▓ R O S E
N O R M A N ▓ P R I N T O U T
T R E A T S ▓ S A M E H E R E
O D E N S E ▓ E Y E S O R E S
```

54

```
P R E A M B L E ▓ C A S S I S
A U N T I E E M ▓ O R I E N T
G R E E N T E A ▓ C A N T D O
E A R N ▓ T R I C K L E S I N
S L O O P Y ▓ L A Y ▓ A C E
▓ ▓ ▓ E B B E D ▓ M E D A L
O P E N R O A D ▓ D E B A T E
L I V E D O N ▓ D O N A T E S
D R E W U P ▓ G O O D N E S S
T A N T E ▓ P A D R E ▓ ▓ ▓
I T S ▓ H I D ▓ F L E W B Y
M I C K J A G G E R ▓ L I R E
E C O L E S ▓ E X A M I N E S
R A R E S T ▓ T I M E Z O N E
S L E E T Y ▓ S T E W A R T S
```

55

```
J E D I M A S T E R ▓ E D N A
A T A B A D T I M E ▓ C O O L
G E T F I R E D U P ▓ Z O N E
S S E ▓ L O R E ▓ L I E N O R
▓ ▓ ▓ J O I N ▓ G A R M E N T
A I R O U T ▓ J A C K A S S ▓
I D E S T ▓ S I Z E S ▓ B E D
M E S H ▓ R I V E D ▓ D E N Y
S A T ▓ B O X E R ▓ P O S S E
▓ L A R I A T S ▓ S O R T E D
A L R E A D Y ▓ O P R Y ▓ ▓
P O T A S H ▓ O B I T ▓ L A W
A V I D ▓ O R D E R A L ▓ I M O
C E N T ▓ G O O S E L I V E R
E R G O ▓ S T R E S S T E S T
```

56

```
J I F F ▓ P U N T A ▓ C A S K
I B A R ▓ I T E M S ▓ A G U E
G E R I ▓ E A M E S ▓ L E N D
S T R E T C H O N E S L E G S
▓ ▓ ▓ N O I ▓ ▓ ▓ S R O ▓ ▓
M I N D O N E S P S A N D Q S
I C E L ▓ G L E A M ▓ T O U T
N A V Y ▓ T I N G E ▓ H E I R
K N E W ▓ O A T E N ▓ E T T A
S T R I N G S A T T A C H E D
▓ ▓ T O E ▓ ▓ ▓ R D A ▓ ▓ ▓
O P E N S T H E D O O R F O R
R A R E ▓ H O V E L ▓ P O L O
Z I N S ▓ E W E L L ▓ E X I T
O D E S ▓ R E N T S ▓ T Y N E
```

57

```
I S I D O R . . T E A P O T
N A V A H O S . M A N M A D E
Q W E R T Y K E Y B O A R D S
U S H . O C E A N U S . L I T
E T A S . E D N A S . T O T E
S A D T O . . . . O N R Y E
T R I P L E T H R E A T . . .
S S T . E L E M E N T . A P E
. . H A I R O F T H E D O G
L O R E N . . . S A V O R
O V A L . H I G H C . T I L E
G I T . B U M M E R S . S A S
J E E P E R S C R E E P E R S
A D D E D T O . R E T I R E E
M O R A S S . . K A N S A S
```

58

```
S C O T . B A C K P E D A L S
T O U R . E C O N O M I C A L
A R T Y . S E M I D I V I N E
P R O S . I D E S . L A D E D
L I F T E D . T H A I . . .
E G O . N E R O . P O M A D E
D E R B Y . O G L E . O R I G
I N D I A N W R E S T L I N G
E D E N . A S I S . Y E S N O
T A R G E T . P E E K . T E N
. . . L O S S . R E S O R T
R I V A L . T W I N . E C T O
A T O M I C P I L E . A R I A
M E L I O R A T E S . T A M S
A M E N T O T H A T . S T E T
```

59

```
G R E A S E S O N E S P A L M
A U G U S T A N A T I O N A L
F R A G R A N C E S T R I P S
F A D . S L Y E . E E L S
E L S A . O I L E D . . .
. . R C A . N O X . H O S E
M I M E O G R A P H P A P E R
A L I T T L E L E A R N I N G
T A K E S A D I S L I K E T O
E Y E S . R A F . E X E . .
. . B E N E T . R S V P
C A R A . T O R E . K O A
H U M A N G U I N E A P I G S
S T O P G A P M E A S U R E S
T E S T S O N E S M E T T L E
```

60

```
S N A I L M A I L . S T A G Y
T O S C A N I N I . S U P R A
L O S E S O N E S T E M P E R
E N I D S . U P T O . I L E D
O S S . E R S T . A L D E N S
. . T A R E . L A D E . P B A
S H A G . D A Y O . S P I E L
T O N E R O W . U K E L E L E
U L T R A . L A T E . O A T S
D E E . G A S P . N A T L .
H I D O U T . R I T Z . A Y N
O N I T . A S I N . T E M P T
R O T T E N T O T H E C O R E
S N O O T . A R E A C O D E S
E E R I E . B I R D S N E S T
```

61

```
T U R G E N E V . E N G I R D
O N E O N O N E . L E A N E R
S L E D D O G S . D A R K L Y
H A L . S K I T T E R . B E E
I C E D . S N E E R . C L A Y
B E R R A . E D S . C H O S E
A S S E S S . I T E R A T E D
. . S K I N N Y D I P . . .
H O U S E C A T . T E E T E R
A C R E D . M E R . S L I C E
M A G S . Z E R O S . S M U G
I R E . R O S E B U D . B A R
T I N M A N . S E R E N A D E
U N C A G E . T R E M O L O S
P A Y E E S . S T R I V E R S
```

62

```
H E I D I G A M E . S I D L E
I N F A V O R O F . O T O E S
P H O N E B I L L . V E R D I
P A R K S . E A S E . M I A
I N G E . T V S T A R . A N S
E C O . R O O T . L E A N T O
S E T S H O T . S T I L T O N
. . P I K E . A L G A . . .
F M B A N D S . G E N E S I S
T O O T O O . N E S S . E N L
R N A . C W M O S S . S A F E
I T T . E N O S . C H L O E
L A M A R . L O S E H E A R T
E N E R O . D A L L I A N C E
Y A N K S . S P O O N F E E D
```

63

```
G R E E K G O D . C T S C A N
P E T P E E V E . A R C A D E
A N T I E T A M . S E A M U S
S E A . P O L O . K R E B S
. . I S U . L O O S E R . .
R E E D I T . I M P . D A M E
O N S E T . S T I E S . L A P
B E C A U S E I T S T H E R E
I R A . P E P O S . A A N D E
N O D S . T I N . C R I S I S
. . R A S H A D . A B R . .
A L I V E . E S S O . B A S
S O L I D S . R O T A T O R S
E U L O G Y . B R E R B E A R
S T E R E S . Y A R D A R M S
```

64

```
S T R A F E D . T S H A P E D
P R O R A T A . S O I L A G E
L U P I N E S . E N L A R G E
I D E E S . H G T . O N T A P
N E S S . G H O S T . S I N S
T A I . P R O B E R S . A D E
S U N B E A M S . E T A L I A
. . . A N N E . B L O B . .
A R M A N I . T E L L S O F F
S O U . I T S A L I E . N O L
H U T S . E U R O S . F A R O
A T A L E . B O W . A O R T A
M I N E R A L . P U L L O U T
E N T E N T E . A A M I L N E
D E S K S E T . R E S O L E D
```

65

```
SEWS GIANTPANDA
AVON ONYOURFEET
DEMO ONEANOTHER
INBRED SHEP IRA
ESTEEMS SIMS
 TORNOUT NETTLE
BET YODEL NOHOW
AVOW DANES PETE
REMAP NOVEL RUR
ENBLOC REVERES
 TRAM REDATES
SOW SCAB NATHAN
TRENCHCOAT TETE
ALLTHERAGE AREA
BYTHEDOZEN NERD
```

66

```
MASONJARS IBARS
ASKSFORIT LOFAT
STILLLIFE SATYR
KATO TALE AREWE
 DESILU DRAT
SNIPED NYSE TLC
PECAN OGDENNASH
EVASION ARTISTE
CENTERSON ACTOR
IRR DEAD LIKENS
ASEA OLDPAL
LOLLY ESAU BALM
OFAGE NARROWTIE
PETAL ORDERARMS
SWEEP WESLEYANS
```

67

```
COMBOS DASCHLE
UVALUE SIMOLEON
RECAST CSIMIAMI
ERASE PRATE DES
APRS LEERY ROIL
LAO HIRAM DONNE
LINEITEM FIB
DISHESTHEDIRT
 TAR HARDNEWS
MOTET DECRY TOA
ALEE JERKY PUSS
YER DUMAS PERTH
DOCTORUP CORNEA
ALEATORY CREEPY
YELPERS RECESS
```

68

```
GRAYAREAS LIMBO
RETICENCE IDEAL
AFTERNOON TITLE
DIALED USO GHIA
ENIDS PSEUD ANN
DENS PETITIONED
 MINI MOROSE
RAYMONDCHANDLER
IMELDA GONE
BASKETFULS HATS
RNS MARIE RERUN
ODIC SAT GALAXY
AIROF PALAVERED
SNEER PROMENADE
TEENY ESCALATOR
```

69

```
CUBFANS GOESBAD
ONECROP ORVILLE
MASCARA GRANULE
PIT BATHES KEMP
ODIC SHUT FEE
TENOF EMTS ULAN
EDGARD BEERNUTS
 CORALREEF
DONTMOVE PARTOF
INES POPS LEOVI
SES NILS EEEE
HISS GLEANS HRS
ROMANIA NETCOST
ATANEND TRIPLEA
GANGWAY STRIDES
```

70

```
BASEBOARD MIMES
APPLETREE ANITA
DALMATIAN TAMAR
ETA HELPME ZOLA
RHYMERS OSMOSIS
 YEARS MTSINAI
 DOO COHERES
 GIVEN
 LEARNER HEF
GOALIES BOLLA
HAARLEM DOLLOPS
RUTH GALAXY ROE
OCHOA TIMESSIGN
SHELF IMPRESSED
SEDER CASSETTES
```

71

```
ITSONME SAFEBET
MRCLEAN AWESOME
PAIDOFF LAMPOON
ODE NIAGARA STU
RENE ANODE STIR
TICKS TOO STEVE
SNEEZE DITHERED
 DEEPSLEEP
ENROLLEE ADOPTS
SEOUL ENG SNARK
SWAT ARSON ELIA
EMS CSLEWIS EFT
NOTDONE ENTITLE
COERCES STARTER
ENDEARS THREERS
```

72

```
ACADEMICDEGREES
NATURALRESOURCE
TRANSPLANTATION
ENL TSETSES SLA
SELL GAIT
 APPL POOR
AFISHOUTOFWATER
DISCONCERTINGLY
DEMANDATTENTION
 LESS SAGE
GAGA EACH
AVA ABANDON MRE
REVOLUTIONARIES
DRESSTOTHENINES
ASLOOSEASAGOOSE
```

73

```
. L O P . M A M B A . S R A S
B A R R . U S U A L . K A R T
A C C O U N T S P A Y A B L E
H E A T P R O S T R A T I O N
. . . E C O . . . M O E . . .
A P B S . . D E R . . S A S S
M E L T I N O N E S M O U T H
A P A S S A G E T O I N D I A
D I S A S S I M I L A T I N G
O N E G . . E Y E . . H O E S
. . . A B R . . . A M I . . .
A C T I V E V O L C A N O E S
R O U N D H O U S E R I G H T
T A B S . A T T A R . C O U P
S L A T . B E S T S . E D D .
```

74

```
F E T I N G . . . N A S C A R
A V E N U E Q . N A M E O N E
M I S S Y O U . A T A C L I P
I D S . S I E S T A S . L O L
N E E D . D E C A L . B E N E
E N R O N . N I L . S E E I T
S T A T E A S S I S T A N C E
. . . E A S E . E K E D . . .
T W O D R I N K M I N I M U M
M I N O S . G I A . S N A K Y
O R A N . I L L I N . G R E W
B E D . D O I T N O W . I L O
I M A R E T S . E D A S N E R
L A T I F A H . S A V E A L L
E N E M Y S . . . T E A S E D
```

75

```
M U S C L E C A R . A F L A T
O N T H E M O V E . C R A T E
D I A L T O N E S . R A S T A
E X T O R T . R E P E N T E R
. . . R I E L . T R A C I N G
D A V I D S O N . A G E N D A
I N A N E . S A O N E . L A S
M I C E . D I D O K . F I N S
I M A . N U N E Z . W I N C E
N A T R O N . R E T I R E E S
I L I E S C U . D I N E . . .
S P O T W E L D . D E C A M P
H E N I E . C A M I S O L E S
E L E N A . E D I E A D A M S
S T R A T . R O S S P E R O T
```

76

```
A L L I G A T O R . J A M E S
C E A S E F I R E . I R A Q I
T A B L E L E A F . V E N U S
A G E . D A R N . R E A T A S
B U L B . T O G G E D . R B I
L E E R S . D E E T . W A L E
E R R A T A . F L Y P A P E R
. . . H A Z A R D P A Y . . .
P R I M R O S E . E L O P E S
R E D S . R I E N . S U A V E
O T C . C E N S O R . T R A C
T I A R A S . T H O U . F S U
E N R O N . F A I R S F A I R
A U D E N . A T T E N T I V E
M E S S Y . Y E S M A S T E R
```

77

```
R A T A T A T . A W N I N G S
A C E T O N E . G R A D U A L
T H R O W I N T O A T I Z Z Y
P E R M S . H A R P O . Z E N
A S I S . B O L A S . M L L E
C O N . F L U K E . F E E L S
K N E E L E R S . D O W S E S
. . . L E S S . T I R E . . .
P A S T E S . S A L A D B A R
A B H O R . A P P L Y . E R E
C A A N . D E A R Y . N E R D
E L M . C U R I O . P O L A R
C O M E R A I N O R S H I N E
A N E M O N E . M U S I N G S
R E D U C E S . S E T T E E S
```

78

```
W E R E T O A S T . C H I C O
A V A L A N C H E . R E H A B
S A W A C T I O N . E R O S E
H C H . T O N O . C O O P E R
O U I S . P U T S O N . E L L
F E D U P . S S N S . E S A I
F E E B L E . D U M B D O W N
. . . M E D I A B I A S . . .
I N H I D I N G . C R E P E D
F I A T . C A G E . I L E N E
O C R . A T T E N D . S T A S
R E P A S S . R D A S . N B A
G O O U T . A S I R E C A L L
E N O T E . H A V E W E M E T
T E N O R . S T E R N N E S S
```

79

```
R E D Y E . D O D I . J A I L
S L O O P . E N V S . U L L A
V I R U S . L C D S . M I L S
P A Y A T T H E P U M P G A S
. . . N E H I . L E P A N T O
L A D D I E . S A D A T . . .
B L O W N A W A Y . A T T I C
O A T H . X A X E S . H E M O
S W O O P . F O R E B E A R S
. . . S E V E N . P A C K E T
S I S E N O R . B A Y H . . .
E Z P A S S T O L L L A N E S
T A U R . T H R O . E N A M I
H A M M . O I N K . A C T I N
S K Y Y . K N E E . F E L L S
```

80

```
C H I N A S E A S . A N I M A
A I D E D A N D A B E T T E D
S H O W I N G O N E S H A N D
T O S E E D . S E T . . L A O
. . . R U B E . . A S S I G N
S H E . X A X I S . M I C E .
P U N T . N A D A . U L T R A
A G R A . K L E I N . L Y I N
S H O R T . T A L E . S P E D
. L L D S . S L O P S . E S S
G A L O O T . R A T A . . . .
Y U M . . A H A . L O G S I N
P R E S S C O N F E R E N C E
S I N K T O O N E S K N E E S
Y E T I S . F O R E S T E R S
```

81

```
S L I P P E D I N   A H E M S
H I R E A L I M O   R E T I E
I V O R Y S O A P   C L A N S
P E N S   A N N A   H E L G A
M A G I C       R H E N I U M
E L A S T I C S   I R A I S E
N I T T Y G R I T T Y
T E E S   O U T I E   S O C A
      S T E A M S H O V E L
S T A B A T   R E T I C E N T
N I C O L A S       M I R T H
A N T A L   H A W S   A R E O
I S I T I   A A R O N B U R R
L E V E E   F R E D A L L E N
S L E D S   T E N S P E E D S
```

82

```
P R I V A T E J E T   R A P T
R O S E P A R A D E   A T O R
E X T R A L A R G E   D O R A
P I L A T E     E N G I N E D
S E E N   N B C   S E C E D E
      D O T E R S   R A T O N
C L E A N E D U P   I L I V E
L E X   A D A M A N T   M E W
O G I L L   U P R O O T E R S
S A T I E   B E E T L E
E L L E R Y   T S E   L U T E
S C A T T E R   P A S T O R
H O N E   T A K E A C T I O N
O D E S   I V I E D H A L L S
P E S T   S I D E S T R E E T
```

83

```
H O T N U M B E R   C R I S P
G A M E T A B L E   T E N O R
T H E M I S S U S   S P A R E
S U N O C O   S I R   O B E S
      A N Y O N E   S A L E
A P A T   S U R   F E E D O N
C A C A O   K Y S E R   S S T
U P T E M P O   T R A P P E D
T E O   A R N I E   T H O R A
E R N A N I   N E W   I T S Y
A M E R   E D E N I C
N O S E   D I R   C H O R A L
G N A T S   G R A C E N O T E
L E G O S   I O W A S T A T E
E Y E O N   T R E N T O N N J
```

84

```
F I B S   H A I R   B R O A D
A T L I   A P P E A L E D T O
R O O D   G O O G L E H I T S
F L O E       R O S A N N E
E D D A   A S C E N T S
T Y S   S T A T S   H E L D
C O U P   P O R T O   I V A R
H U G O   R S A   N E N E
E S A I   A M E B A   G N A W
D O R N   S C A L D   C T A
      T A K E T E A   T H U S
C H E E R O N   E A R P
H O L D B U T T O N   A N N A
E S S A Y T E S T S   C C E D
F E A T S   R E B A   H E R E
```

85

```
S O R D I D   Z A N Z I B A R
O N I O N Y   E P H E M E R A
B A G G I E   R O L E P L A Y
E L A M   S T O L E S   A B O
R E T A B   N C A R   K I L N
S A O   A P O O R   H A R E S
U S N   R S T U   J A R
P H I L L I E P H A N A T I C
      Y E S   O R I G   R S A
C A M R Y   E N O L A   U N S
O S E E   D E B S   R H E T T
V E X   M O R O S E   A G H A
E V I L T W I N   N E U R O N
R E C E S S E D   D E L I M E
T R O T T E R S   S E S T E T
```

86

```
S O M E T H I N G S F I S H Y
A P A S S A G E T O I N D I A
P I C T U R E P O S T C A R D
    E Y E R   T A S   I K E A
    V I T A L   E S T
A F R E S H   I N N U E N D O
B A E Z   I N S I D E   A R B
E T D   I N A   N U T   D U E
A S I   D I P P E R   A I R Y
M O D E L C A R   E S S A Y S
      V E E   A N D E S
B I L E   L E O   A U L D
I S I N A R O T T E N M O O D
R E F U S E T O R E C E I V E
D E E P E S T R E C E S S E S
```

87

```
H O S T E D   S H O W D O W N
I C H I R O   E U P H O R I A
N E O C O N   C L A I M A N T
D A R K S   Q U A R T I L E S
I N T L   C U R   T E N
  F R E S H A I R   R I D G E
O R A   P O R T I A   C U R T
N O N D A I R Y C R E A M E R
E N G R   R E D H O T   B E E
S T E A M   L E T S D O W N
      M E A   P E E   P A A R
S P R A N G F O R   R E I C H
T O O T S I E S   P A N T R Y
A R T I C L E I   E S T E E M
T E A C H E S T   A H O R S E
```

88

```
S N E A K A P E E K   S F P D
T A M B O U R I N E   P A R E
O N E A N D O N L Y   E X I T
W A R C R I M E S   L A P S E
      K A T E S   M I R R O R
D O M   D E T   B A T H I N G
I V I E   D H L A W R E N C E
S E L M A   E O N   E A T E N
T R I A L J U D G E   D E L T
R E T I L E S   L U C   R L S
E X I L E D   H A T H A
S C A L Y   H I D E A W A Y S
S I M I   W A T E R P I P E S
E T A S   W H I S P E R I N G
D E N T   I N T H E L E A S T
```